ENHANCED EDITION

ALL-IN-ONE PIANO COURSE
Lessons • Technique • Theory

ADULT PIANO *Adventures*® *by Nancy and Randall Faber*

1

Production Coordinator: Jon Ophoff
Cover: Terpstra Design, San Francisco
Engraving: Dovetree Productions, Inc.

FABER
PIANO ADVENTURES®

ISBN 978-1-61677-302-1

Welcome

New to the Piano?

This book offers musical instruction that will guide you as a beginning adult learner. Over two hours of instructional video provide a professional perspective to accelerate your musical training. Supporting audio tracks convey a sonic world of rhythm, melody and harmony — essential for learning musical concepts.

Enhance your learning with instructional videos by world-renowned pianist and educator Randall Faber.

Returning to the Piano?

If you had piano lessons previously, this is your refresher course. You may move quickly through Book 1, but take your time with the video content of each unit. You'll gain deeper understanding and find an expressive dimension in your playing.

Energize your Brain!

New and familiar melodies, basic music theory, creative exploration, and expressive playing provide stimulation and enrichment!

How This Book is Organized

You will study 16 units, each covering a new concept while providing review of previous topics and skills.

Concepts are displayed in a shaded file folder.

Practice suggestions guide your first steps.

Discovery questions invite deeper analysis and creative activities engage your brain in new ways.

Optional teacher duets provide a steady beat and a rich sound.

QR codes give immediate video access to each piece, play-along orchestrations, and a unit summary video with Randall Faber.

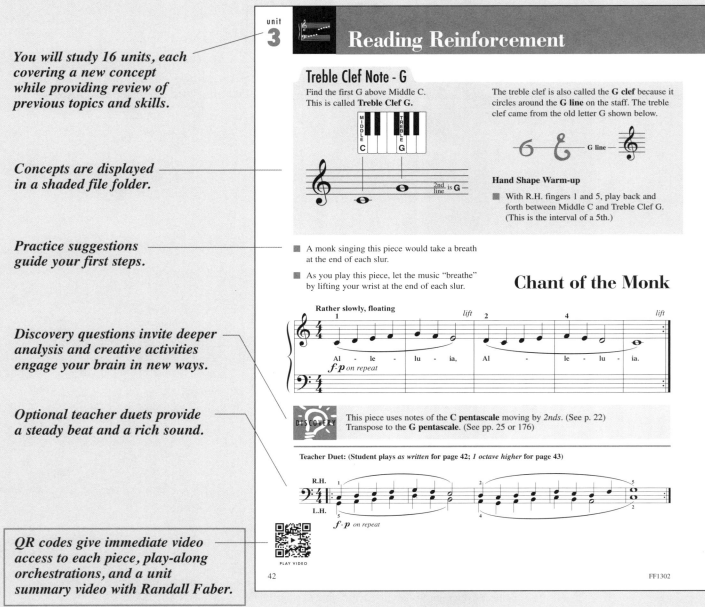

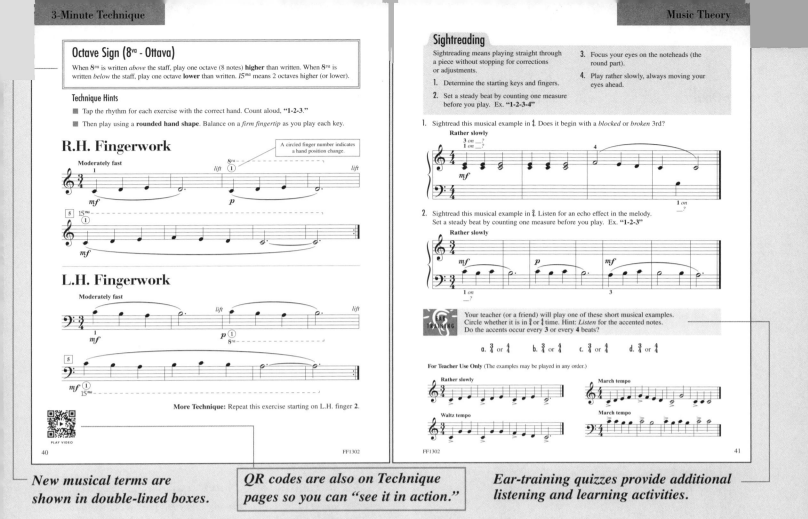

New musical terms are shown in double-lined boxes.

QR codes are also on Technique pages so you can "see it in action."

Ear-training quizzes provide additional listening and learning activities.

At the end of each unit, you will find a 3-Minute Technique page and a Music Theory page. Technique pages develop an optimal physical approach to the piano, and build finger dexterity in just three minutes a day. Music theory activities help you learn chords and harmony while increasing your reading skills.

Enhanced Audio Support

Download the Piano Adventures Player® app for interactive accompaniment tracks that adjust to any speed. Fun and easy to use!

Expand your repertoire!

Play dozens of familiar songs at just the right level in the Adult Piano Adventures supplementary books. Choose among your favorite genres, including Popular, Classics, and Christmas.

Contents

THE PIANO

The piano is perhaps the world's most celebrated instrument. The standard acoustic piano boasts a range of sound that encompasses the longest string of a booming low A to the shortest string of the highest C, a dynamic range of hushed *pianissimo* (very soft) to thunderous *fortissimo* (very loud), and a unique capacity to play any number of notes at the same time.

The piano is a veritable orchestra at our fingertips. Since its invention around 1700 by Bartolomeo Cristofori, the piano has evolved to a magnificent instrument with over 10,000 parts.

Strings – Today's piano uses high tension steel for the strings. There are three strings for each key, except in the bass (lower) register where there are two strings per key or a single string wrapped in coiled copper. The pitch of a string is determined by its length and tension. The higher tones have shorter strings, while lower tones may have strings over three feet in length.

The strings of a grand piano are horizontal, whereas an upright piano utilizes vertical strings to save floor space.

Keys – The standard piano keyboard spans 88 keys. The key mechanism resembles a seesaw, with each key being a lever. As the key is struck, a hinged hammer on the other end comes up to strike the strings. At the moment of impact, the key also lifts the damper off of the strings, allowing the string to continue to vibrate. The white keys, formerly made of ivory, are plastic on today's piano. The black keys, formerly of ebony, are usually constructed of stained pear wood.

Hammers – The hammers (located underneath the strings) are covered with felt. The volume of sound is determined by the speed of the hammer striking the string.

To play louder, the hammer must strike the string faster. To play softer, the hammer must strike the string slower.

Escapement – The most brilliant and revolutionary feature of Cristofori's early piano was the escapement. This escapement action allows the hammer to fall away immediately after striking the string, thus letting the sound ring. Through continued improvements, the escapement in the modern piano makes rapid repetition of a key possible.

Soundboard – The soundboard is located below the strings (behind the strings on an upright piano). The soundboard amplifies the tone of the vibrating strings through sympathetic vibration. Cracks can develop in the soundboard due to dryness or extreme temperature changes. Humidity control and stable temperatures preserve the health of the soundboard.

Pedals – Pianos have two or three pedals. The damper pedal (the pedal to the right) is used most often. It lifts the dampers off the strings, sustaining the sound until the pedal is released. The damper pedal adds a soulfulness to melodies, a richness to harmonies, and a shimmer to fast passagework.

The *una corda* or "soft pedal" (left pedal) shifts the keyboard to the right, causing the hammers to strike one fewer string. In addition to softening the sound, the *una corda* pedal changes the tone quality to a more muted, veiled sound.

If a piano has a *sostenuto* pedal, it is the pedal in the middle. The *sostenuto* pedal sustains the sound of those keys depressed when the pedal goes down. Notes played after this are not sustained. The *sostenuto* pedal is not essential for playing the piano repertoire.

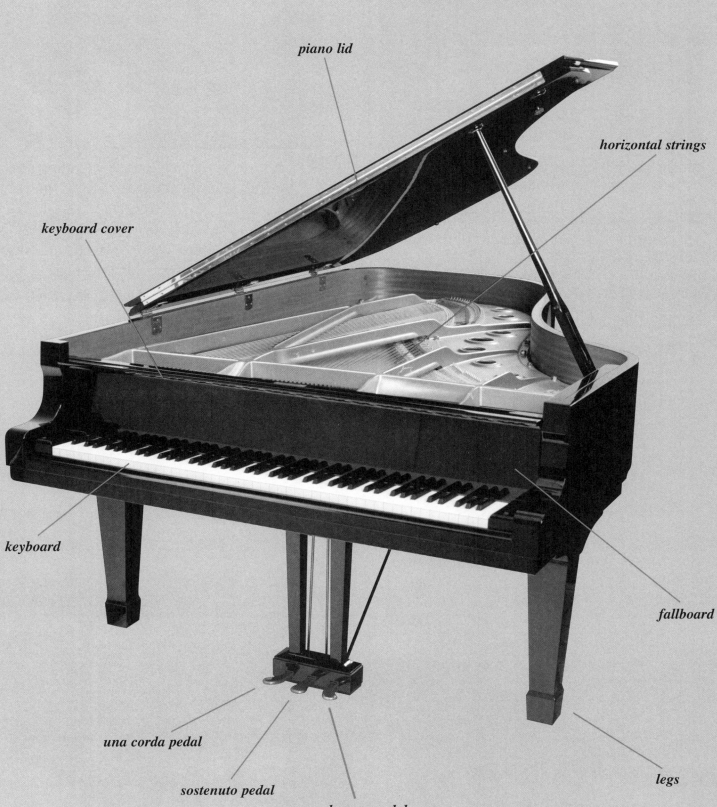

piano lid

horizontal strings

keyboard cover

keyboard

fallboard

una corda pedal

legs

sostenuto pedal

damper pedal

Introduction to Playing

Posture at the Piano

Distance

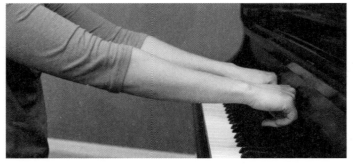

- Sit straight on the front half of the bench with your body weight balanced.

- With your arms extended out, **your knuckles should reach the fallboard**. If you have to lean, move the bench forward or backward.

Hand Position

ROUNDED Hand Position

Thumb plays on the side tip

- Let your arms hang loosely at your sides. Notice the **natural curve** of your fingers.

- Now gently place your hands on the keys.

  It is important to keep a relaxed, **rounded hand position** as you play the piano.

Seating Height Check

1. With shoulders relaxed, place your hands on the keys.

2. **Your forearms should be level with the keyboard**. Adjust your seating height up or down.

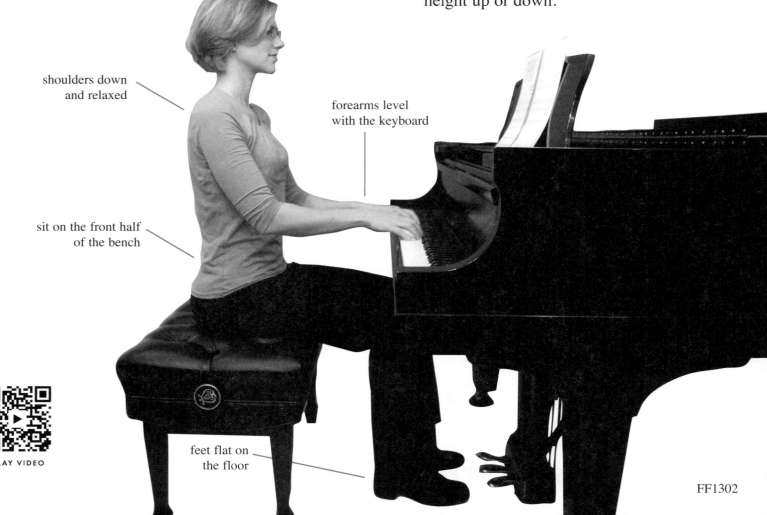

shoulders down and relaxed

forearms level with the keyboard

sit on the front half of the bench

feet flat on the floor

PLAY VIDEO

FF1302

Finger Numbers

Each finger is given a number—1, 2, 3, 4 and 5. The thumb is finger 1.

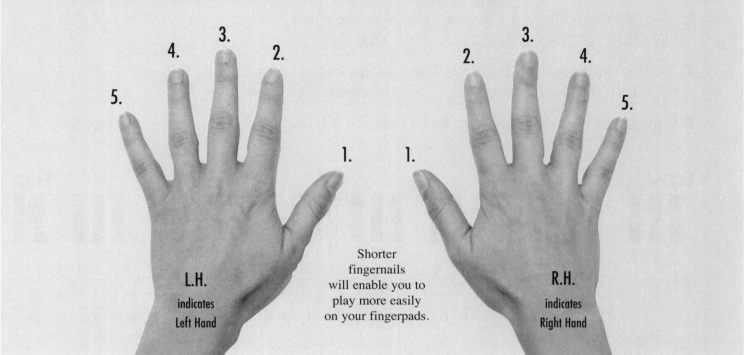

L.H.
indicates
Left Hand

Shorter
fingernails
will enable you to
play more easily
on your fingerpads.

R.H.
indicates
Right Hand

Finger Number Warm-ups

■ Place your hands in a *rounded hand position* on your lap.

Gently "scratch" **finger 1s** (thumbs),
finger 2s,
finger 3s,
finger 4s,
finger 5s.

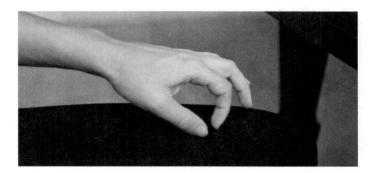

■ With a **rounded hand position** and **firm fingertips**, choose any white key.
Play it with RIGHT HAND finger 1, then 2, 3, 4, and 5.
Now reverse, starting with finger 5.

Hint: *Play the thumb on the side tip.*

■ Then, with a rounded hand position and firm fingertips, choose any white key.
Play it with LEFT HAND finger 1, then 2, 3, 4, and 5. Now reverse.

High and Low on the Keyboard

The piano KEYBOARD has white keys and black keys. Notice the black keys alternate between groups of **two** and **three**.

■ Silently touch all the 2-black-key groups on the piano.
Use L.H. for lower groups and R.H. for higher groups.

■ Now silently touch all the 3-black-key groups on the piano.
Use L.H. for lower notes and R.H. for higher notes.

■ Now close your eyes. Can you find a group of 2-black-keys? A group of 3-black-keys?

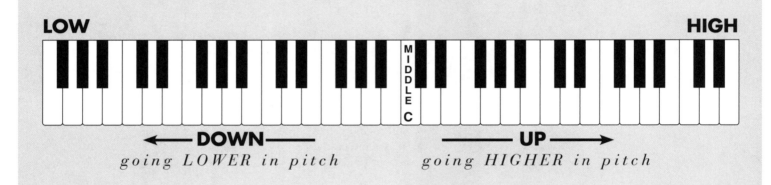

Soft and Loud on the Keyboard

The keys on the piano can be played softly or loudly, with many variations in between.
Let's begin with these two basic tones:

p = *piano*   The Italian word for soft, quiet.

f = *forte*   The Italian word for loud. (Pronounced FOR-tay.)

Raindrops for R.H.

R.H. fingers 2-3 on a 2-black-key group

Damper pedal

1. Begin and end in the MIDDLE of the keyboard. Use R.H. fingers 2 and 3 together.
   Play the 2-black-key groups going UP, then back DOWN the keys (higher, then lower).

2. Play *piano*. Sink gently into the keys. Lift gently from the wrist as you move across the keys.

3. Now play and **depress the damper pedal** (right foot pedal) **throughout**. Keep your heel on the floor and your foot in contact with the surface of the pedal. Listen to the sound!

Thunder for L.H.

L.H. fingers 2-3 on a 2-black-key group

Damper pedal

1. Begin and end in the MIDDLE of the keyboard. Use L.H. fingers 2 and 3 together.
   Play the 2-black-key groups going DOWN, then back UP the keys (lower, then higher).

2. Play *forte*. Drop with the weight of your arm for a deep, rich tone.

3. Now play and **depress the damper pedal** (right foot pedal) **throughout**. Listen to the sound!

DISCOVERY   Repeat *Raindrops* and *Thunder* using fingers 2-3-4 on the **3-black-key** groups.

PLAY VIDEO

Review of Finger Numbers (See page 9)

- Numbers below the words indicate L.H. fingers.
  Numbers above the words indicate R.H. fingers.

- Extended lines in the lyrics show held tones.

- The dots show quickly moving tones.
  Let your familiarity with the melody help guide you.

Hand Placement

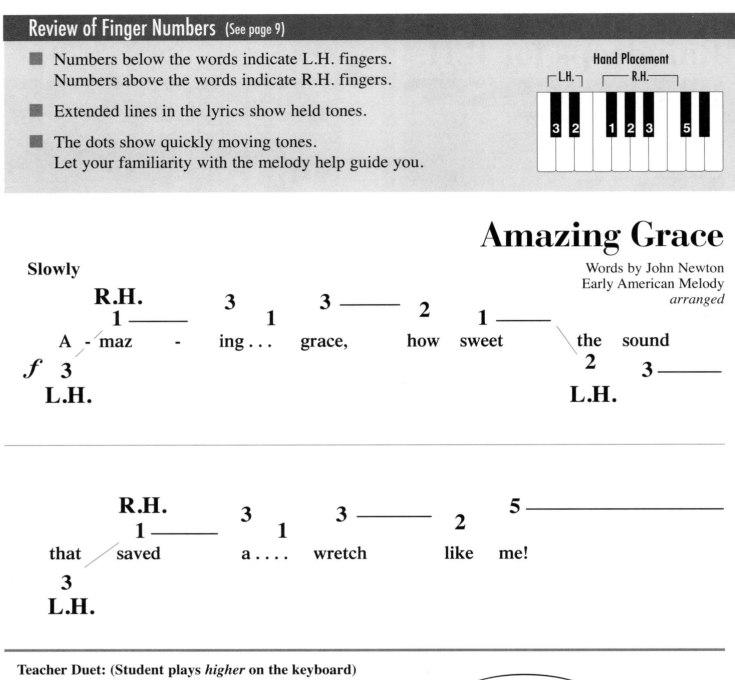

Amazing Grace

Words by John Newton
Early American Melody
arranged

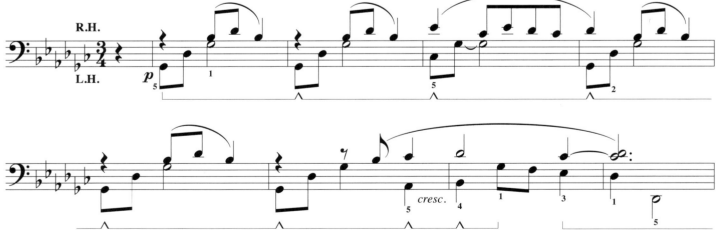

Teacher Duet: (Student plays *higher* on the keyboard)

FF1302

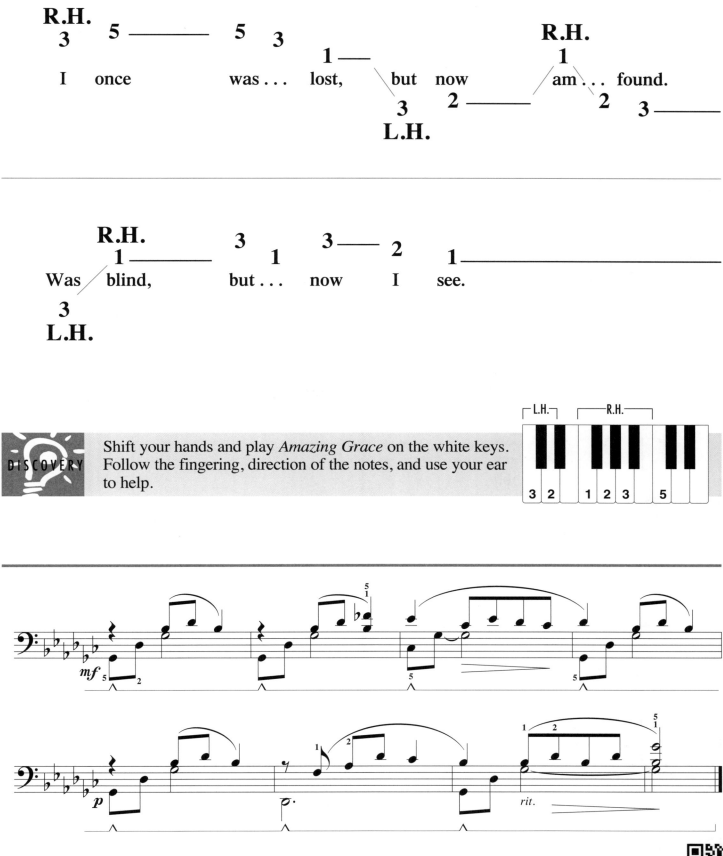

R.H.

3   5 —— 5   3

             1 —

I   once   was . . . lost,   but   now

R.H.

1

       am . . . found.

            3   2 ——   2   3 ——

L.H.

R.H.

1 ——   3   1   3 —— 2   1 ———————

Was / blind,   but . . . now   I   see.

3

L.H.

Shift your hands and play *Amazing Grace* on the white keys. Follow the fingering, direction of the notes, and use your ear to help.

PLAY VIDEO

Rhythm

Note values indicate the duration of the sound.

These durations are counted with a steady beat, creating RHYTHM.

You may wish to use a **metronome** for the Rhythm Chart below.

A metronome is a rhythmic device that provides a steady beat. Adjustable settings allow a faster or slower beat.

■ Tap (or clap) the Rhythm Chart from top to bottom, counting aloud.
  Feel a steady beat (♩ = 100). Each click represents a quarter note.

■ Choose any white key and play the notes in the Rhythm Chart from top to bottom, then bottom to top. Use finger 3.

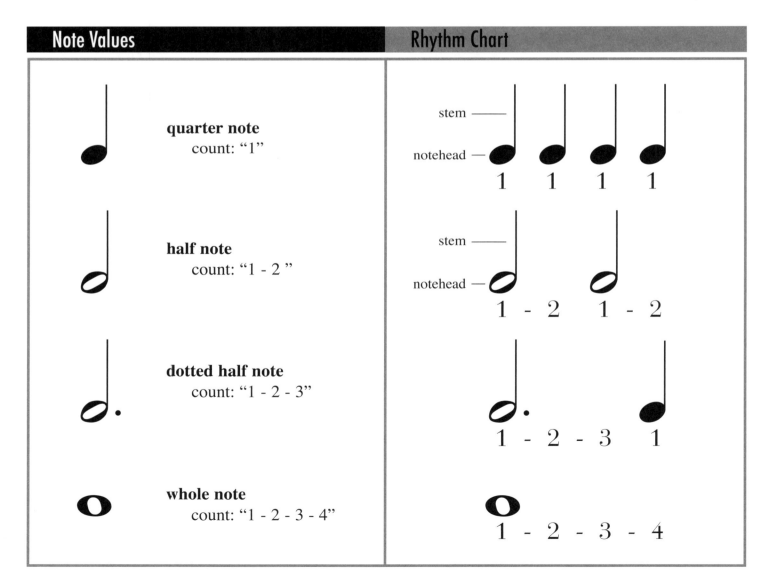

Note Values	Rhythm Chart
quarter note count: "1"	stem — notehead — 1 1 1 1
half note count: "1 - 2"	stem — notehead — 1 - 2 1 - 2
dotted half note count: "1 - 2 - 3"	1 - 2 - 3 1
whole note count: "1 - 2 - 3 - 4"	1 - 2 - 3 - 4

FF1302

■ Tap the rhythm of this piece on the closed keyboard cover with the correct hand.

    L.H. = stem down   R.H. = stem up

■ Playing *in the middle* of the piano, say or sing:
a. finger numbers **b.** counts **c.** words

Hand Placement

Morning
(from *Peer Gynt Suite No. 1*)

Edvard Grieg
(1843-1907, Norway)
arranged

Double bar line means the end of the piece.

Teacher Duet: (Student plays *higher* on the keyboard)

PLAY VIDEO

White Key Names

Each white key has a letter name from the music alphabet: **A B C D E F G**

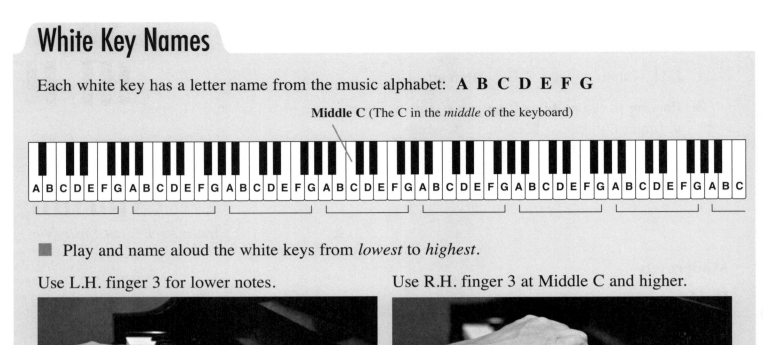

Middle C (The C in the *middle* of the keyboard)

■ Play and name aloud the white keys from *lowest* to *highest*.

Use L.H. finger 3 for lower notes.

Use R.H. finger 3 at Middle C and higher.

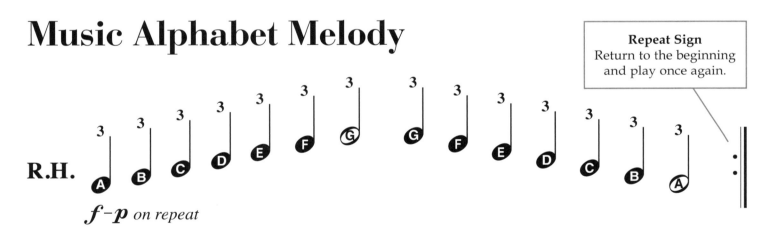

■ Find an "A" in the *middle* of the keyboard. (Look for the three-black-key group. The **A key** is *between* black keys two and three.)

■ Play and sing the music alphabet up and down. Use R.H. finger 3.

Music Alphabet Melody

Repeat Sign
Return to the beginning and play once again.

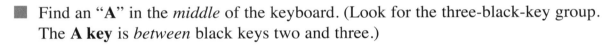

R.H.

f-p on repeat

Teacher Duet: (Student plays *higher* on the keyboard)

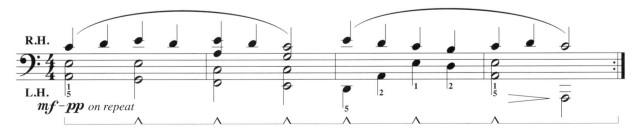

mf-pp on repeat

FF1302

Use the 2-black-key group to locate C-D-E.

Think: D is in the middle of the 2-black-keys. "Hey diddle-diddle, D's in the middle."

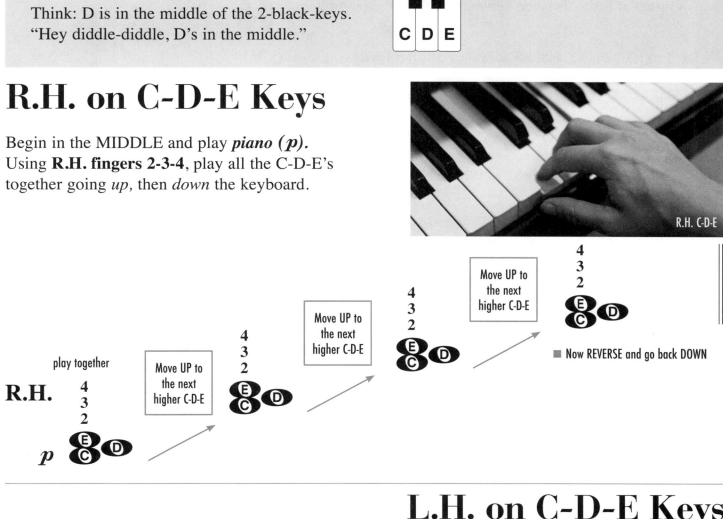

R.H. on C-D-E Keys

Begin in the MIDDLE and play *piano (p)*.
Using **R.H. fingers 2-3-4**, play all the C-D-E's together going *up*, then *down* the keyboard.

R.H. C-D-E

play together

R.H. 4 3 2

p (E)(C)(D)

Move UP to the next higher C-D-E

4 3 2
(E)(C)(D)

Move UP to the next higher C-D-E

4 3 2
(E)(C)(D)

Move UP to the next higher C-D-E

4 3 2
(E)(C)(D)

■ Now REVERSE and go back DOWN

---

f (D)(E)(C)
2 3 4

L.H.

play together

Move DOWN to the next lower C-D-E

(D)(E)(C)
2 3 4

Move DOWN to the next lower C-D-E

(D)(E)(C)
2 3 4

L.H. on C-D-E Keys

Begin in the MIDDLE and play *forte (f)*.
Using **L.H. fingers 4-3-2**, play all the C-D-E's together going *down*, then *up* the keyboard.

Move DOWN to the next lower C-D-E

(D)(E)(C)
2 3 4

■ Now REVERSE and go back UP

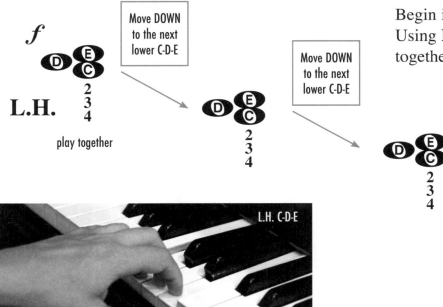

L.H. C-D-E

PLAY VIDEO

Interval

An **interval** is the distance between two keys, including the *first* and *last* key.

Ex. From C up to E is the interval of a **third (3rd)**. The interval of a third spans three letter names.

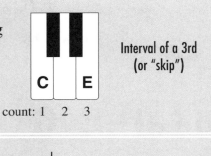

Interval of a 3rd (or "skip")

count: 1 2 3

Blocked or Broken

An interval can be played broken (separately) or blocked (together).

R.H. Interval Warm-up

R.H. C-E

Begin in the MIDDLE. Use **R.H. fingers 1-3**. Depress the damper pedal and play C and E *broken*, then *blocked*. Go higher and higher up the keyboard. Play *forte* (***f***).

■ Repeat with R.H. fingers **2-4** on C and E.

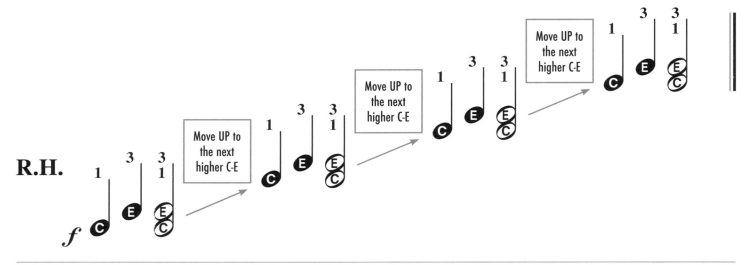

R.H.

Move UP to the next higher C-E

L.H. Interval Warm-up

Begin in the MIDDLE with **L.H. fingers 3-1**. Use pedal and play C and E *broken*, then *blocked*. Go lower down the keyboard. Play *piano* (***p***).

■ Repeat with L.H. fingers **4-2** on C and E.

PLAY VIDEO

FF1302

■ Tap (or clap) the rhythm, counting aloud.

■ Playing *in the middle* of the piano, say or sing:
a. finger numbers   **b.** letter names   **c.** counts

(Say the higher finger number or letter name for the *blocked 3rds*.)

Merrily We Roll Along

Traditional

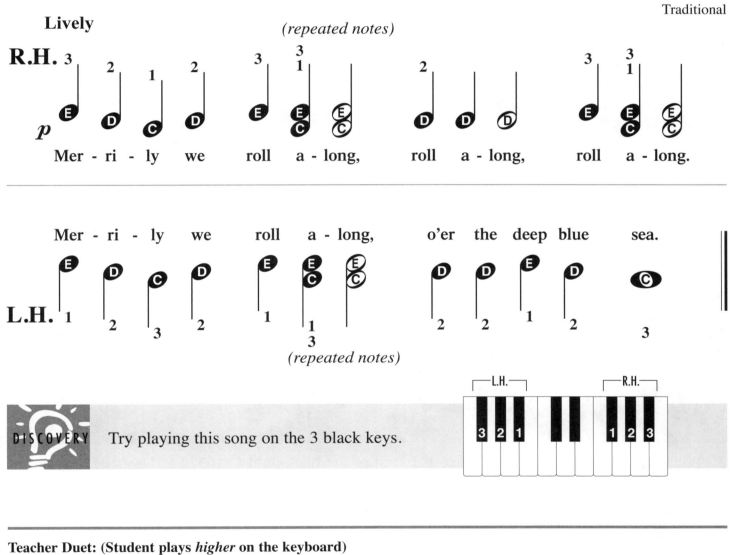

DISCOVERY   Try playing this song on the 3 black keys.

Teacher Duet: (Student plays *higher* on the keyboard)

PLAY VIDEO

Learning F-G-A-B

Use the 3-black-key group to locate F-G-A-B.

F-G-A-B on the Keys

1 L.H. on F-G-A-B

1. Begin in the MIDDLE. Play *piano (p)*. Using **L.H. fingers 5-4-3-2**, play all the **F-G-A-B's** together going *down*, then *up* the keyboard.

2 R.H. on F-G-A-B

2. Begin in the MIDDLE. Play *forte (f)*. Using **R.H. fingers 2-3-4-5**, play all the **F-G-A-B's** together going *up*, then *down* the keyboard.

3 L.H. on F-A

3. Begin in the MIDDLE of the keyboard. Use **L.H. fingers 3** and **1**. Depress the damper pedal and play F and A *broken*, then *blocked* going lower and lower down the keyboard. Play *forte (f)*.

  ■ Repeat using L.H. fingers **4** and **2** on F and A.

4 R.H. on F-A

4. Begin in the MIDDLE. Use **R.H. fingers 1** and **3** on F and A. Depress the damper pedal and play F and A *broken*, then *blocked* going higher and higher up the keyboard. Play *forte (f)*.

  ■ Repeat using R.H. fingers **2** and **4** on F and A.

Transposing

Playing the same piece using different keys is called transposing. On page 19, you played *Merrily We Roll Along* using keys C-D-E. On the next page, *Merrily We Roll Along* is transposed to keys F-G-A.

The Measure

A *measure* is a group of beats.
Measures within the same piece usually have the same number of beats.

Bar lines divide the music into measures.
Keep the rhythm flowing smoothly *over* the bar lines.

■ Study the musical example below.

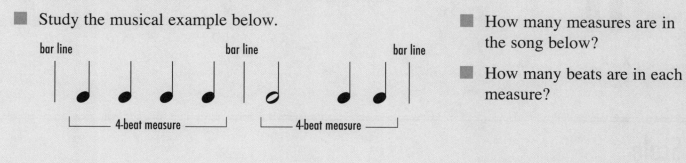

■ How many measures are in the song below?

■ How many beats are in each measure?

■ Tap (or clap) the rhythm, counting aloud.

■ Playing *in the middle* of the piano, say or sing:
a. finger numbers   **b.** letter names   **c.** counts

(Say the higher finger number or letter name for the *blocked 3rds*.)

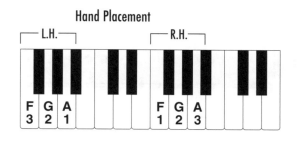

Hand Placement

Merrily We Roll Along

Traditional

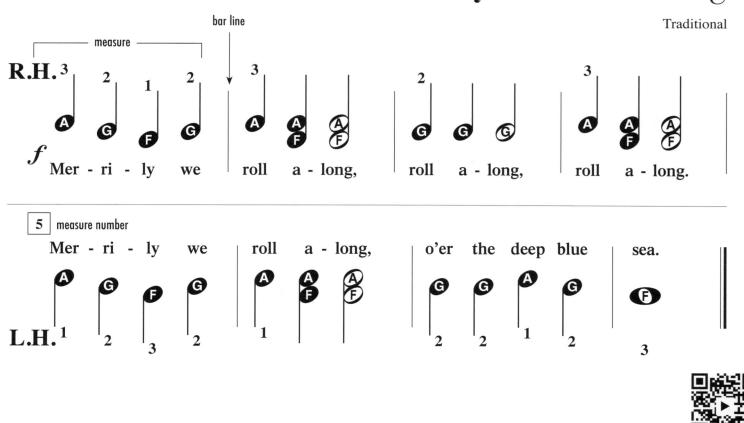

Seconds (2nds)

Remember, an *interval* is the distance between two keys.

The interval of a **2nd** moves up or down to the:
next KEY — next LETTER NAME — next FINGER

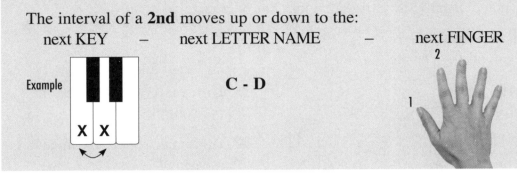

Example

C - D

Scale

The word **scale** comes from the Latin *scala*, meaning "ladder." The notes of a scale move up or down by **2nds** (steps). *Penta* is Latin for "five." A pentascale is a 5-note scale.

◼ Place R.H. fingers in the **C Pentascale**.
Play up and down. Sing **C D E F G F E D** C.

◼ Playing *in the middle* of the piano, say or sing:
a. finger numbers **b.** letter names **c.** counts

◼ **Transpose** to *higher* and *lower* C Pentascales.

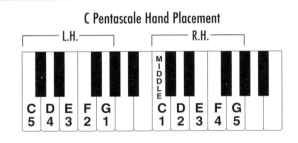

C Pentascale Hand Placement

Keep the quarter notes steady.

C Pentascale Warm-up

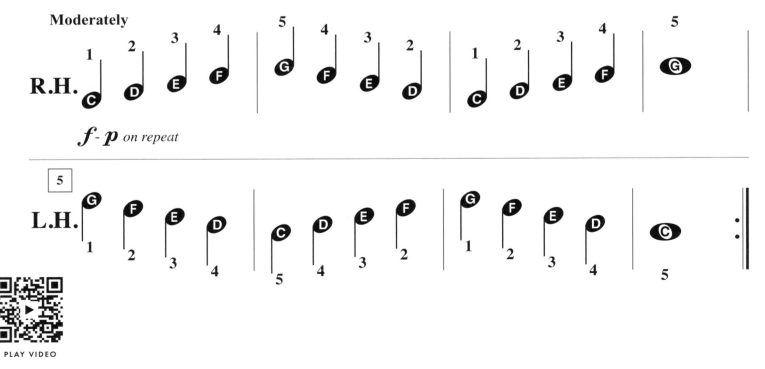

Moderately

f - p on repeat

Thirds (3rds)

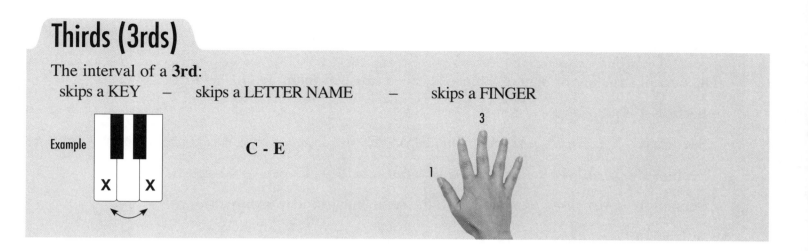

The interval of a **3rd**:

skips a KEY   –   skips a LETTER NAME   –   skips a FINGER

Example

C - E

- This piece uses **broken 3rds** in the C scale. Depress the damper pedal throughout.

- Playing *in the middle* of the piano, say or sing:
  a. finger numbers   **b.** letter names   **c.** counts

- **Transpose** to *higher* and *lower* C Pentascales.

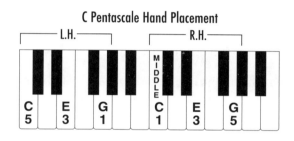

C Pentascale Hand Placement

Warm-up with 3rds

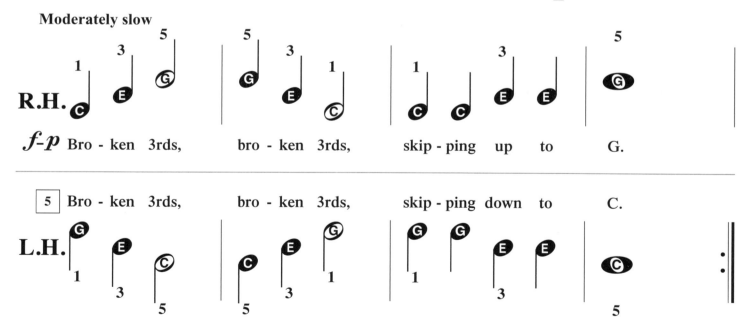

Moderately slow

R.H.

f-p Bro - ken 3rds,   bro - ken 3rds,   skip - ping up to G.

5 Bro - ken 3rds,   bro - ken 3rds,   skip - ping down to C.

L.H.

CREATIVE   Depress the damper pedal. Play any blocked or broken **3rds** *high* on the keyboard. *Listen* to the sound of 3rds.

PLAY VIDEO

Musical Form

The overall structure or plan of a piece is called **musical form**. In *Ode to Joy*:

Section A – *Measures 1-4* can be labeled **A**.

Section A¹ – *Measures 5-8* can be labeled **A¹** because in *measure 8* it is changed slightly from **A**.

Section B – *Measures 9-12* present a new musical idea and can be labeled **B**.

Section A¹ – *Measures 13-16* return to the same musical idea as *measures 5-8*.

The form of *Ode to Joy* is **A A¹ B A¹**.

■ Circle all the **repeated notes**.

■ Playing *in the middle* of the piano, say or sing:
a. finger numbers   **b.** letter names

■ Label each section of the musical form in the boxes below.

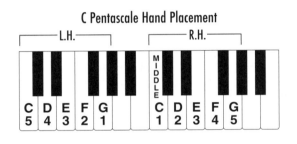

C Pentascale Hand Placement

Ode to Joy
(Theme from the 9th Symphony)

Ludwig van Beethoven
(1770-1827, Germany)
arranged

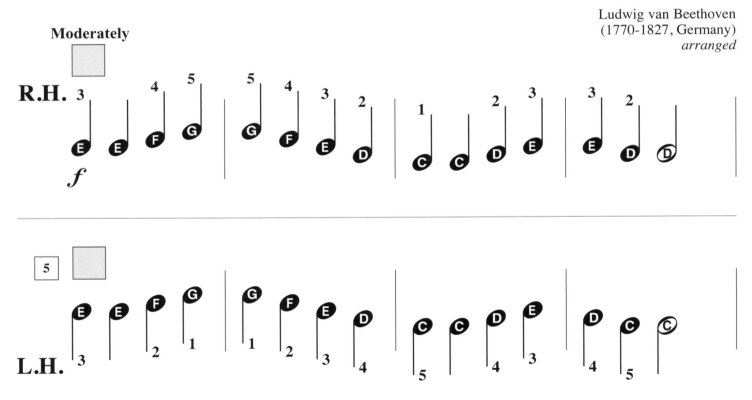

PLAY VIDEO

FF1302

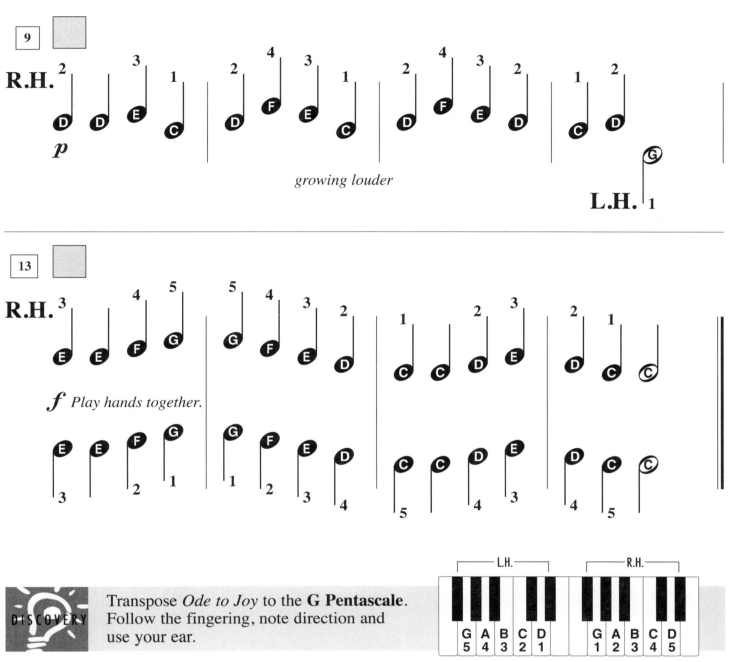

growing louder

Play hands together.

Transpose *Ode to Joy* to the **G Pentascale**.
Follow the fingering, note direction and
use your ear.

DISCOVERY

G Pentascale Hand Placement

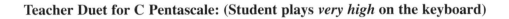

Teacher Duet for C Pentascale: (Student plays *very high* on the keyboard)

Dynamic Marks

Remember **p** is soft, **f** is loud. (See p. 10)
These are called **dynamic marks**.

mezzo forte (*mf*)

means moderately loud
(pronounced MET-tsoh FOR-tay)

Musical Pattern

A *musical pattern* that is repeated higher or lower on the keyboard is called a **sequence**.

■ For each exercise, start *in the middle* of the piano.

R.H. Study in 2nds and 3rds

Moderately

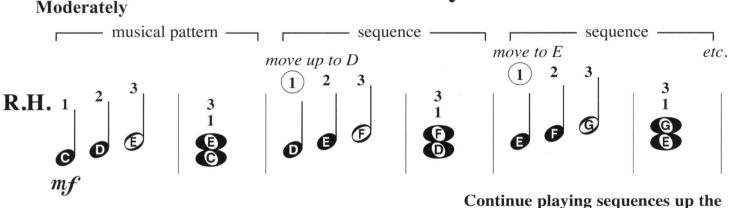

**Continue playing sequences up the
white keys on F, G, A, B, and C.**

L.H. Study in 2nds and 3rds

Moderately

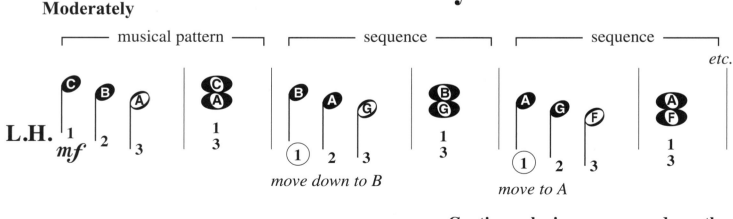

**Continue playing sequences down the
white keys on G, F, E, D, and C.**

PLAY VIDEO

FF1302

1. Review of 2nds and 3rds

■ Review **2nds** and **3rds** by naming the keys marked with an X.

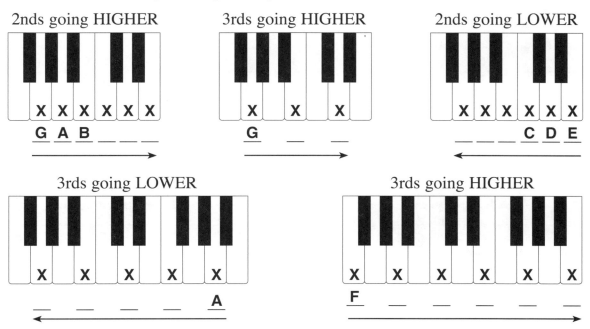

2nds going HIGHER

G A B _ _ _

3rds going HIGHER

G _ _

2nds going LOWER

_ _ _ C D E

3rds going LOWER

_ _ _ _ A

3rds going HIGHER

F _ _ _ _ _

2. Rhythm Tap

■ Tap this two-handed rhythm on the closed keyboard cover while counting aloud. Your R.H. taps the *top line* while your L.H. taps the *bottom line*. (Your teacher will demonstrate.)

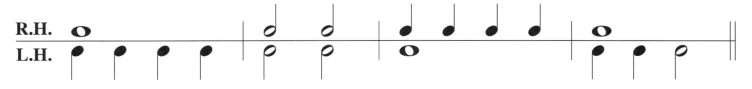

R.H.

L.H.

3. Black-Key Improvisation

To improvise is to create "on the spot."

■ Find a friend or ask your teacher to play the duet part below. First, *listen* and feel the beat.

■ When you are ready, improvise a piece using **only black keys**. Use either hand (or both). There are no right or wrong notes, only music!

Teacher Duet: (Student improvises *higher* on the same keyboard)

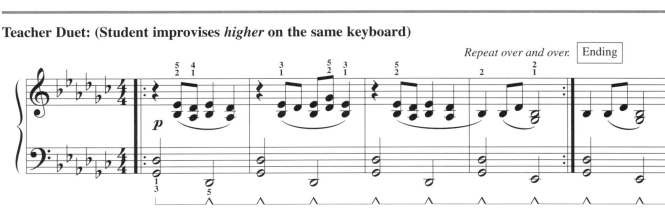

Orientation to the Staff

The Staff

Music is written on a five-line staff.

5
4
3
2
1

Notes are written on **lines** (line notes) or in **spaces** (space notes).

5 Line Notes   **4 Space Notes**

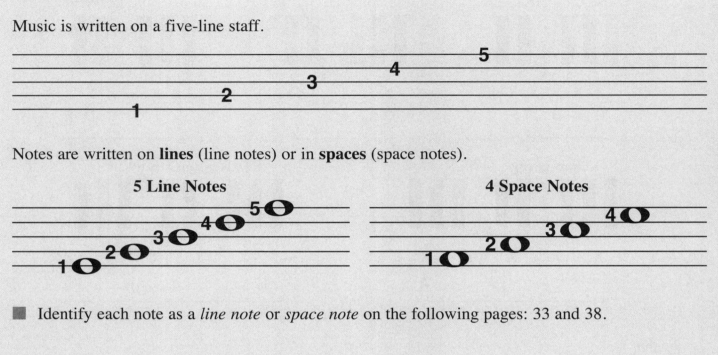

■ Identify each note as a *line note* or *space note* on the following pages: 33 and 38.

The Grand Staff

Piano music uses two staves (staffs) which are connected by a brace and beginning bar line. Together we call them the **GRAND STAFF**.

> The R.H. plays the notes in the *upper* staff.

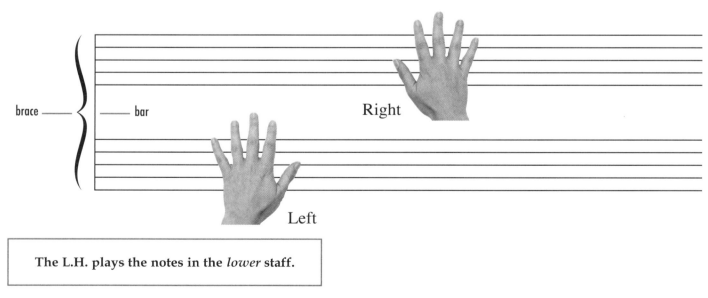

brace —— ⎨ —— bar

Right

Left

> The L.H. plays the notes in the *lower* staff.

PLAY VIDEO

FF1302

Bass Clef and Treble Clef

 This is a **Bass Clef** sign.
Bass refers to *low* sounds.

 This is a **Treble Clef** sign.
Treble refers to *high* sounds.

The bass clef shows notes *below* Middle C.

The treble clef shows notes *above* Middle C.

Bass Clef Orientation

■ With L.H. finger 2, play Middle C and all the keys below while naming them aloud. These are in the *bass clef* range.

Treble Clef Orientation

■ With R.H. finger 2, play Middle C and all the keys above while naming them aloud. These are in the *treble clef* range.

Note: Middle C is written on a *ledger line* (short line) between the treble and bass staves.

The Alphabet on the Staff

■ As notes on the staff move from a **space** to the next **line** to the next **space**, etc., they move by **2nds** (steps) on the keyboard. (See page 34.)

■ How many times can the music alphabet be written on the grand staff? Begin at the bottom and count up. _____

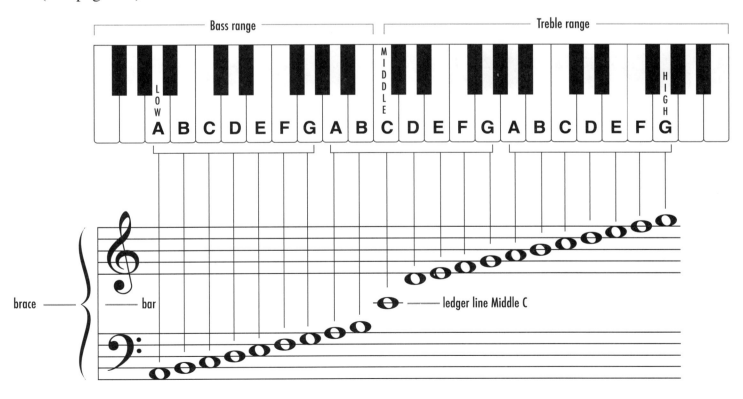

The $\frac{4}{4}$ Time Signature

The **time signature** is written at the beginning of a piece of music.

- The *top* number indicates the number of beats per measure.

- The *bottom* number represents the kind of note receiving one beat.

$\frac{4}{4}$ = 4 beats in each measure ("1-2-3-4")

$\frac{4}{4}$ = ♩ The quarter note receives one beat.

Warm-up

Tap (or clap), counting aloud, **"1-2-3-4"** in each measure. Notice this is a new way to count.

Then choose any key on the piano and play, counting aloud. Use R.H. finger 3.

Count: 1 2 3 4   1 - 2 3 - 4   1 - 2 - 3 4   1 2 3 4

4-Beat Alphabet uses only finger 3.

- First play, saying the **letter names**. (Begin two A's *below* Middle C.)

- Then play, counting aloud, **"1-2-3-4."** Accent (play louder) beat 1 of each measure.

4-Beat Alphabet

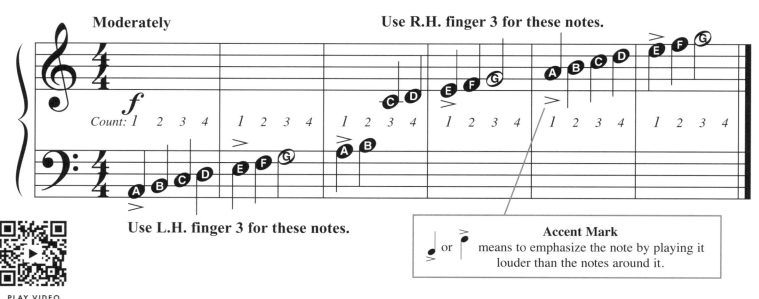

Moderately

Use R.H. finger 3 for these notes.

Count: 1 2 3 4 1 2 3 4 1 2 3 4 1 2 3 4 1 2 3 4 1 2 3 4

Use L.H. finger 3 for these notes.

Accent Mark
♩ or means to emphasize the note by playing it louder than the notes around it.

The ¾ Time Signature

3
4

= 3 beats in each measure ("1-2-3")

= ♩ The quarter note receives one beat.

Warm-up

Tap (or clap), counting aloud, **"1-2-3"** in each measure.

Then choose any key on the piano and play, counting aloud. Use R.H. finger 3.

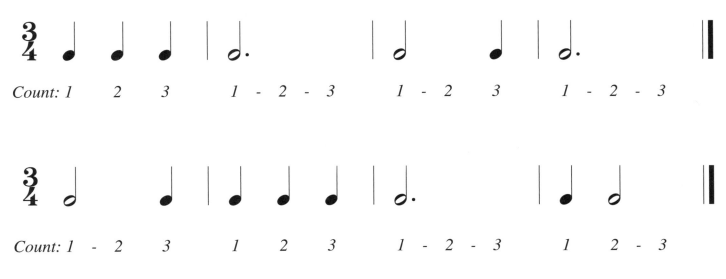

Count: 1 2 3 1 - 2 - 3 1 - 2 3 1 - 2 - 3

Count: 1 - 2 3 1 2 3 1 - 2 - 3 1 2 - 3

■ Now play feeling **3 beats** per measure.

■ Count aloud, **"1-2-3."** Accent beat 1 of each measure.

3-Beat Alphabet

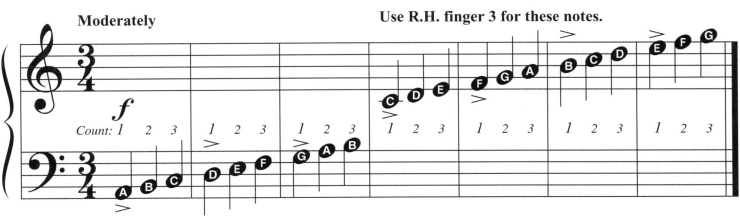

Moderately

Use R.H. finger 3 for these notes.

Count: 1 2 3 | 1 2 3 | 1 2 3 | 1 2 3 | 1 2 3 | 1 2 3 | 1 2 3

Use L.H. finger 3 for these notes.

Play these familiar melodies which use $\frac{4}{4}$ and $\frac{3}{4}$ **time signatures**.
The letter names inside the notes will guide you.

■ Name the **time signature** for each melody.
Write it at the *beginning* of each piece.

■ Playing *in the middle* of the piano, say or sing:
a. finger numbers **b.** letter names **c.** counts

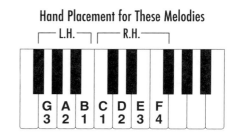

Hand Placement for These Melodies

Yankee Doodle

Traditional

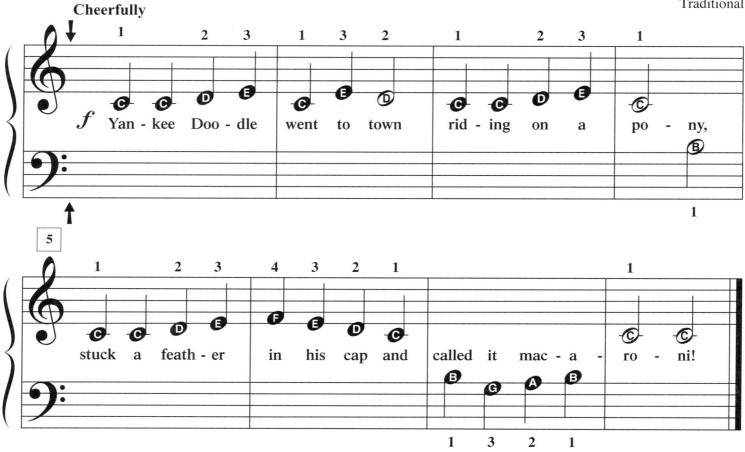

Teacher Duet: (Student plays *1 octave higher*)

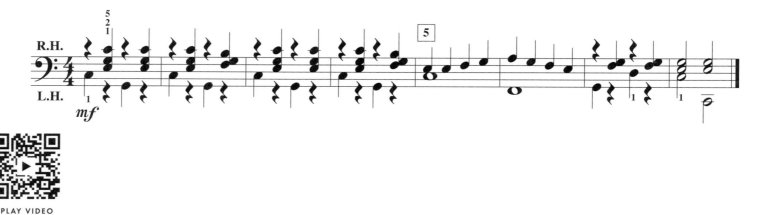

PLAY VIDEO

32

FF1302

■ Tap (or clap) the rhythm for
these 3/4 melodies. Count aloud.

Row, Row, Row Your Boat

Traditional

■ Can you finish the melody to
Row, Row, Row, Your Boat?

Pedal Mark

Pedal DOWN   *hold it down*   Pedal UP

Clock Tower Bells

Traditional

 Transpose *Clock Tower Bells* using
these keys and finger numbers.

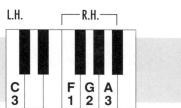

PLAY VIDEO

Reading 2nds (Steps) on the Staff

■ On the staff, the **interval of a 2nd (step)** is from:

a LINE to the next SPACE

line - space

or

a SPACE to the next LINE
(See p. 29)

space - line

■ Learn and memorize these four notes:
B, **C**, **D**, and **E**. Remember, Middle C
is written on a *ledger line* between the
treble and bass staves. (See p. 29)

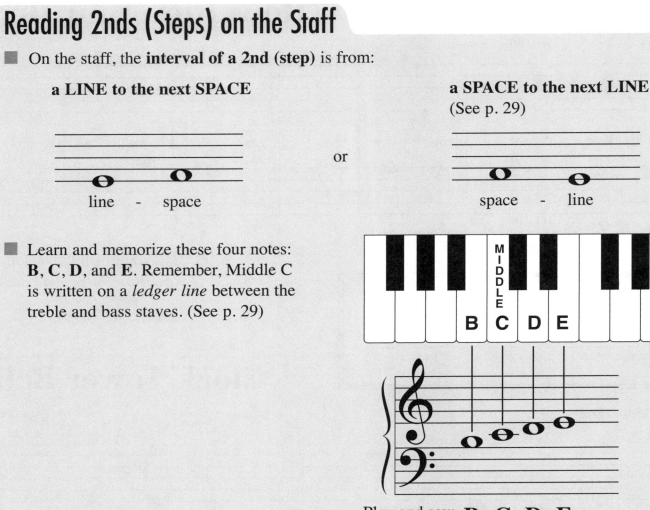

Play and say: **B C D E**
space-line-space-line

Warm-up with 2nds

■ Name each note in the blanks below.

Moderately

f-p *on repeat*

note names: __ __ __ __ __ __ __

The Tie

= 8 beats

The **tie** is a curved line connecting two repeated notes on the *same line* or *space*. The note is played *once*, but held for the length of both notes combined.

Catch a Falling Star

Words and Music by
Paul Vance and Lee Pockriss

Cheerfully

Catch a fall-ing star and put it in your pock-et, nev-er let it fade a - way.

Catch a fall-ing star and put it in your pock-et, save it for a rain - y day.

DISCOVERY Transpose this piece using this set of keys.

Teacher Duet: (Student plays *1 octave higher*, without pedal)

PLAY VIDEO

Bass Clef Note - A

This **A** is the top line of the bass staff.
It is a **2nd** *below* B.

• Play and say: **A B C D E**

line - space - line - space - line

L.H. Warm-up

Moderately   **blocked 3rd**

mf **1** *on* __?

play $\frac{1}{3}$ *together*

Repeat beginning with L.H. finger 2 on C.

■ Tap (or clap) the rhythm. Count aloud, **"1-2-3-4."**

■ Look through the piece, noting the *form:* **A A B B A¹**

■ Play, observing the f, p, and > marks.

Russian Folk Song

Traditional Russian
arranged

With spirit

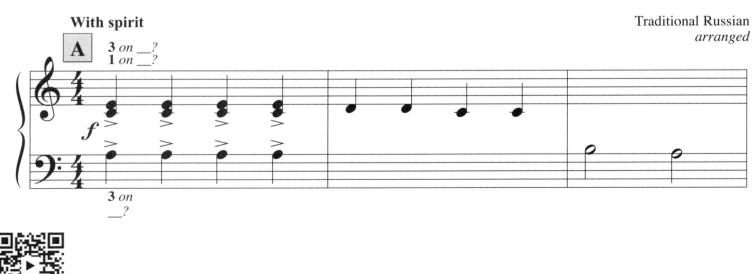

A 3 *on* __?
1 *on* __?

f

3 *on*
__?

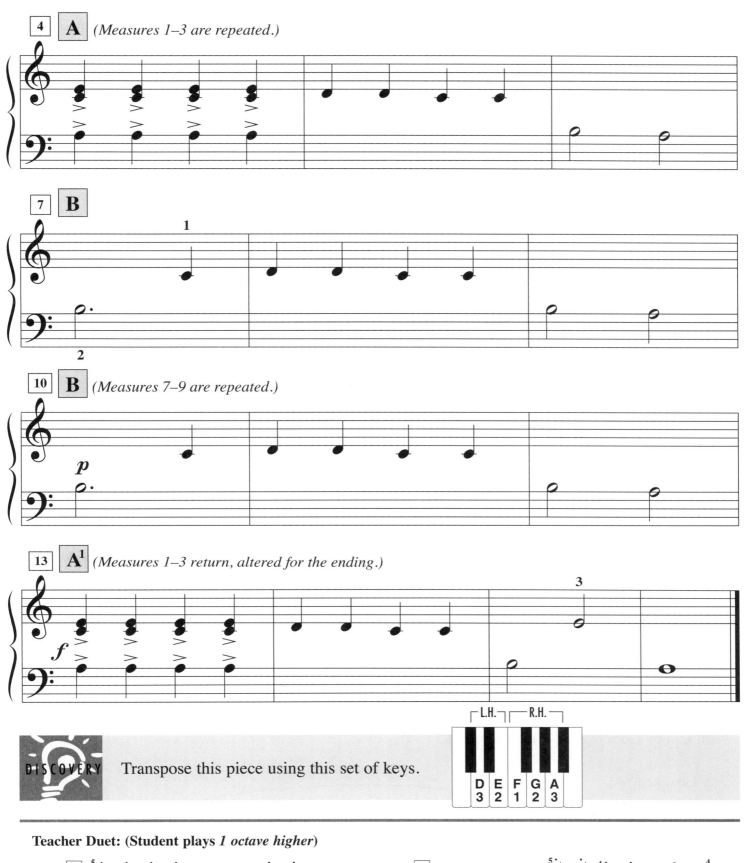

4 **A** *(Measures 1–3 are repeated.)*

7 **B**

10 **B** *(Measures 7–9 are repeated.)*

13 **A¹** *(Measures 1–3 return, altered for the ending.)*

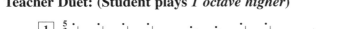

DISCOVERY   Transpose this piece using this set of keys.

Teacher Duet: (Student plays *1 octave higher*)

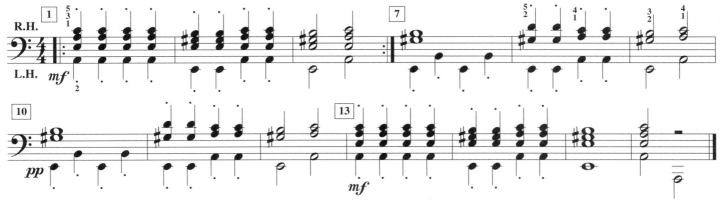

Treble Clef Note - F

This **F** is the first space of the treble staff.
It is a **2nd** *above* E.

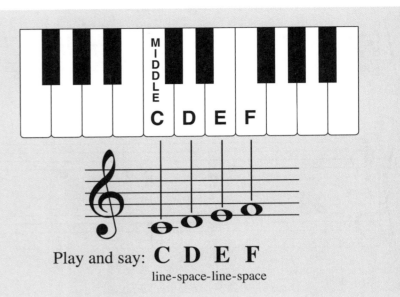

Play and say: **C   D   E   F**
line-space-line-space

Legato

Legato means smooth and connected, with no break in the sound. To play *legato*, one finger goes down as the previous finger releases.

A **slur** is a curved line over or under a group of notes. It indicates *legato*.

■ Play this example. Listen for a smooth, connected sound.

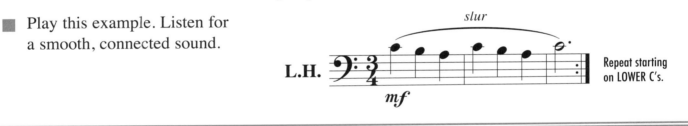

Repeat starting on LOWER C's.

■ Tap (or clap) the rhythm. Count aloud, **"1-2-3."**

■ Count again and tap only on beat 1.

Midnight Ride

Fast, urgent

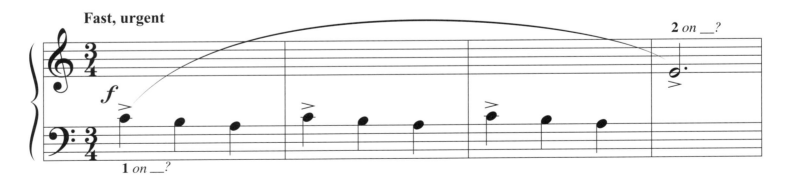

2 on __?

1 on __?

PLAY VIDEO

FF1302

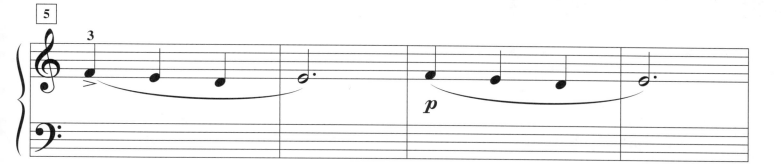

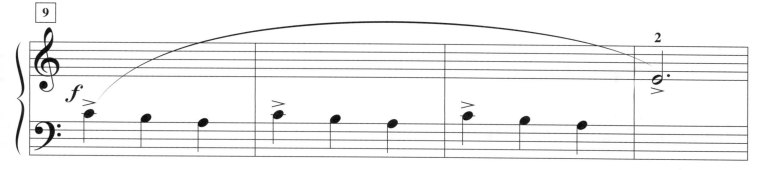

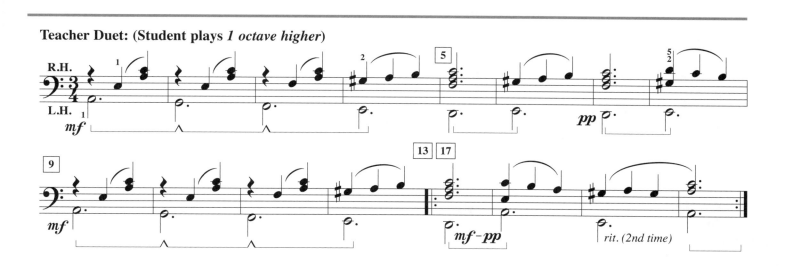

Teacher Duet: (Student plays *1 octave higher*)

Octave Sign (8va - Ottava)

When *8va* is written *above* the staff, play one octave (8 notes) **higher** than written. When *8va* is written *below* the staff, play one octave **lower** than written. *15ma* means 2 octaves higher (or lower).

Technique Hints

▪ Tap the rhythm for each exercise with the correct hand. Count aloud, **"1-2-3."**

▪ Then play using a **rounded hand shape**. Balance on a *firm fingertip* as you play each key.

R.H. Fingerwork

A circled finger number indicates a hand position change.

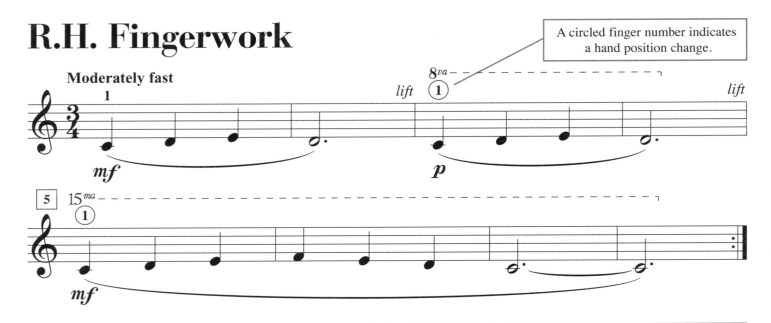

L.H. Fingerwork

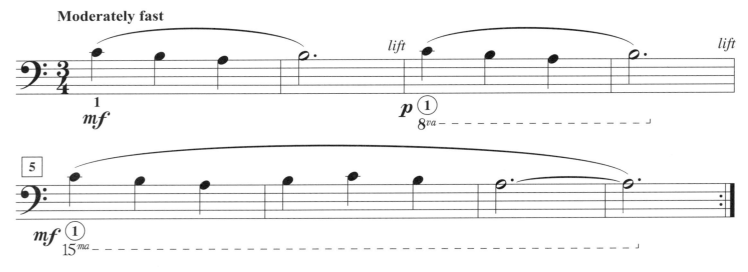

More Technique: Repeat this exercise starting on L.H. finger **2**.

PLAY VIDEO

FF1302

Sightreading

Sightreading means playing straight through a piece without stopping for corrections or adjustments.

1. Determine the starting keys and fingers.

2. Set a steady beat by counting one measure before you play. Ex. **"1-2-3-4"**

3. Focus your eyes on the noteheads (the round part).

4. Play rather slowly, always moving your eyes ahead.

1. Sightread this musical example in $\frac{4}{4}$. Does it begin with a *blocked* or *broken* 3rd?

2. Sightread this musical example in $\frac{3}{4}$. Listen for an echo effect in the melody. Set a steady beat by counting one measure before you play. Ex. **"1-2-3"**

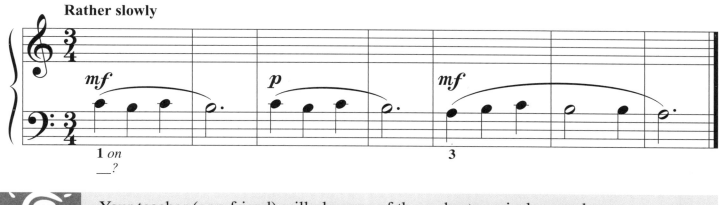

EAR TRAINING Your teacher (or a friend) will play one of these short musical examples. Circle whether it is in $\frac{3}{4}$ or $\frac{4}{4}$ time. Hint: *Listen* for the accented notes. Do the accents occur every **3** or every **4** beats?

a. $\frac{3}{4}$ or $\frac{4}{4}$ b. $\frac{3}{4}$ or $\frac{4}{4}$ c. $\frac{3}{4}$ or $\frac{4}{4}$ d. $\frac{3}{4}$ or $\frac{4}{4}$

For Teacher Use Only (The examples may be played in any order.)

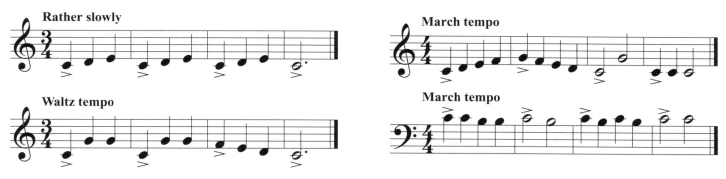

unit 3

Reading Reinforcement

Treble Clef Note - G

Find the first G above Middle C.
This is called **Treble Clef G.**

The treble clef is also called the **G clef** because it circles around the **G line** on the staff. The treble clef came from the old letter G shown below.

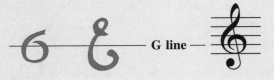

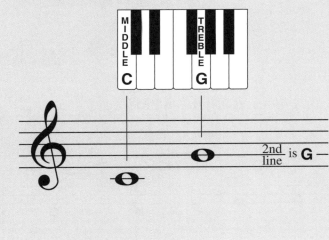

$\frac{2nd}{line}$ is **G**

Hand Shape Warm-up

■ With R.H. fingers 1 and 5, play back and forth between Middle C and Treble Clef G. (This is the interval of a 5th.)

■ A monk singing this piece would take a breath at the end of each slur.

■ As you play this piece, let the music "breathe" by lifting your wrist at the end of each slur.

Chant of the Monk

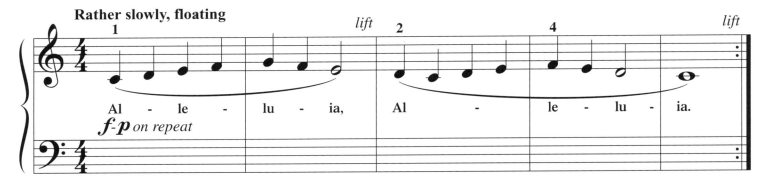

Rather slowly, floating

Al - le - lu - ia, Al - le - lu - ia.

f-p on repeat

DISCOVERY This piece uses notes of the **C pentascale** moving by *2nds*. (See p. 22)
Transpose to the **G pentascale**. (See pp. 25 or 176)

Teacher Duet: (Student plays *as written* **for page 42;** *1 octave higher* **for page 43)**

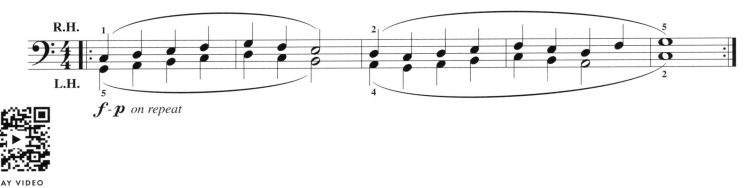

R.H.
L.H.
f-p on repeat

PLAY VIDEO

FF1302

- First play each hand separately. The L.H. will play the same melody using a lower C Pentascale. Listen for a smooth, *legato* sound.

- Now play hands together. Let your R.H. "teach" your L.H. Notice the letter names stay the same, but the finger numbers are different.

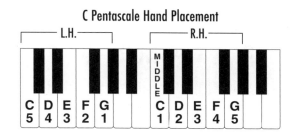

C Pentascale Hand Placement

Chant of the Monks

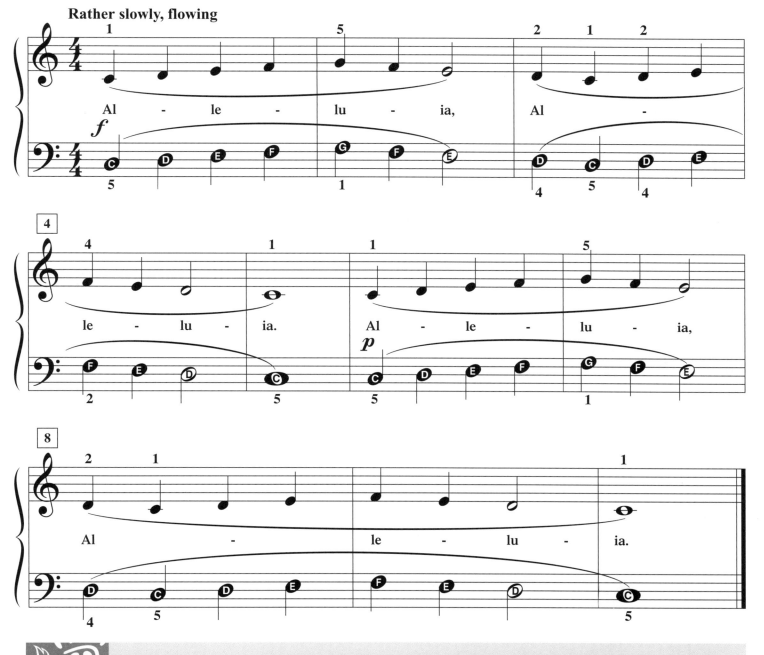

Rather slowly, flowing

Al - le - lu - ia, Al - le - lu - ia. Al - le - lu - ia, Al - le - lu - ia.

Teacher Duet: See bottom of page 42.

Transpose this piece to the **G pentascale**. Then create a short G pentascale "Chant" of your own. Play up or down by **2nds**, hands alone or together.

PLAY VIDEO

Bass Clef Note - G

This **G** in the bass clef is a 2nd (step) *below* A.
It is located on the top space of the bass staff.

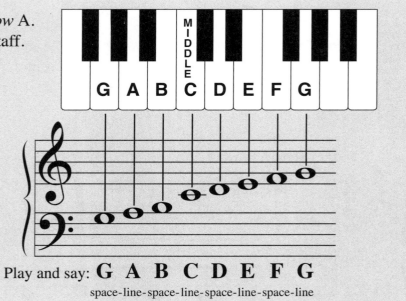

Play and say: **G A B C D E F G**

space-line-space-line-space-line-space-line

■ Before playing, scan the music
and observe the musical form.

Shining Stars

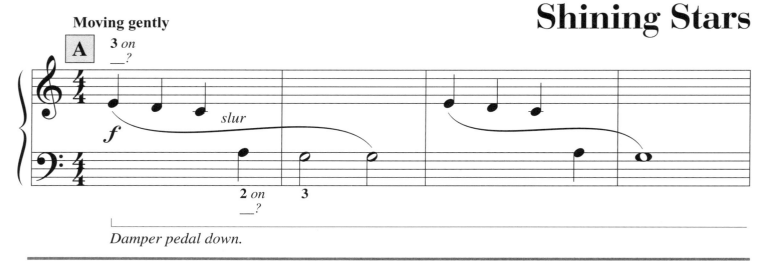

Moving gently

A 3 *on*
___?

f   slur

2 *on*
___?   3

Damper pedal down.

Teacher Duet: (Student plays *1 octave higher*, without pedal)

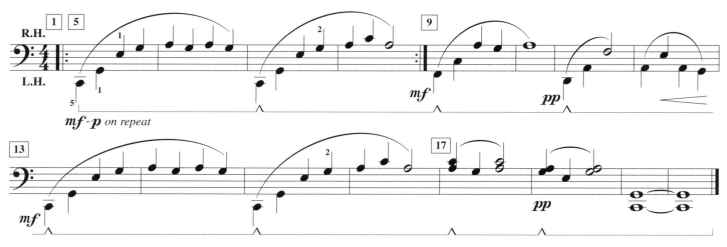

R.H.

L.H.

mf-p on repeat

mf   *pp*

mf   *pp*

FF1302

5 **A**

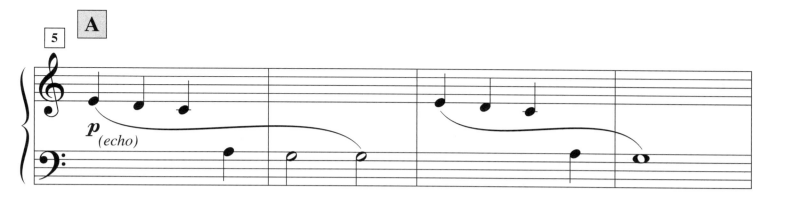

9 **B**

play $\frac{3}{1}$ *together*

play $\frac{2}{3}$ *together*

13 **A¹**

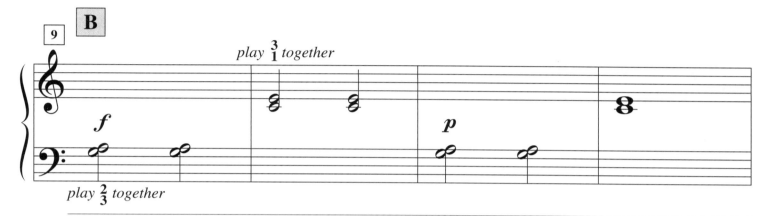

17 **Coda** (ending section)

$\frac{3}{1}$

lift **BOTH HANDS** *lift* **BOTH HANDS**
8va 15ma *(2 octaves higher)*

Play both hands together. *lift* *p* *lift* *as soft as possible*

$\frac{2}{3}$

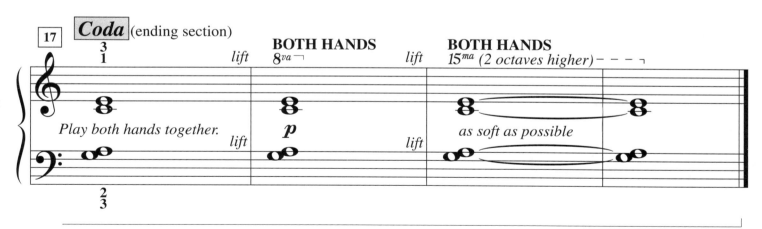

Pedal up.

Point out a **broken 2nd**, **blocked 2nd**, then a **blocked 3rd**.
(Find a broken 3rd in *measure 1*. Look between treble and bass notes.)

PLAY VIDEO

Bass Clef Note - F

Find the first F below Middle C.
This is called Bass Clef F.

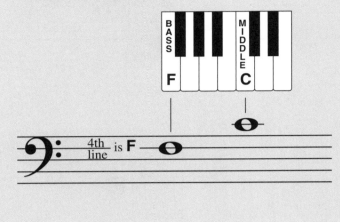

The bass clef is also called the **F clef**. The two dots point out the F line on the staff. The bass clef came from the old letter F shown below.

Hand Shape Warm-up

■ With L.H. fingers 1 and 5, play back and forth between Middle C and Bass Clef F. (This is the interval of a **5th**.)

Musical Form Check

The form of this piece is **A A B A¹**.

■ Label each section in your music.

Roman Trumpets

FF1302

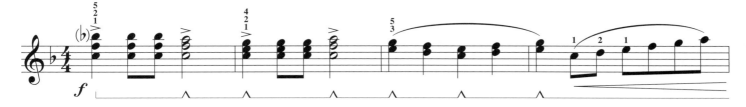

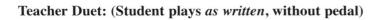

 DISCOVERY Find the following: accent mark, interval of a 5th, and octave sign.

Teacher Duet: (Student plays *as written*, without pedal)

PLAY VIDEO

Tempo

The tempo is the speed of the music.

■ Practice these exercises at a slow, medium,
then faster tempo. Play with firm fingertips.

R.H. Study in 2nds

L.H. Study in 2nds

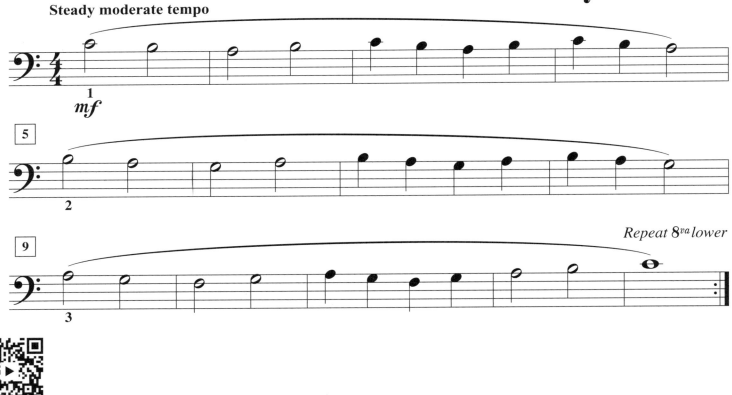

PLAY VIDEO

48

1. For each musical example, circle the correct description:

repeat, 2nd ↑, 2nd ↓
repeat, 2nd ↓, 2nd ↓
2nd ↑, 2nd ↓, repeat

repeat, 2nd ↑, 2nd ↑
2nd ↑, repeat, 2nd ↓
2nd ↑, repeat, 2nd ↑

2nd ↑, 2nd ↓, repeat
2nd ↑, repeat, 2nd ↓
2nd ↓, 2nd ↑, repeat

2nd ↑, repeat, 2nd ↑
repeat, 2nd ↑, repeat
2nd ↑, 2nd ↓, repeat

repeat, 2nd ↓, 2nd ↑
2nd ↓, repeat, 2nd ↓
2nd ↓, repeat, 2nd ↑

2nd ↓, 2nd ↓, repeat
repeat, 2nd ↓, repeat
2nd ↑, 2nd ↓, repeat

2nd ↓, repeat, 2nd ↑
2nd ↓, 2nd ↓, 2nd ↑
2nd ↓, 2nd ↓, repeat

repeat, 2nd ↑, 2nd ↑
2nd ↑, 2nd ↑, repeat
2nd ↑, repeat, 2nd ↑

2nd ↓, 2nd ↑, 2nd ↓
2nd ↓, 2nd ↓, 2nd ↑
2nd ↓, repeat, 2nd ↓

2. Play each example above. Notice the fingering.

3. C Pentascale Improvisation

■ Ask a friend or your teacher to play the duet part below. First, listen and feel the beat.

■ When you are ready, improvise a melody using the **C pentascale** notes (C-D-E-F-G) *in any order.* For rhythmic variety, use longer and shorter notes.

Teacher Duet: (Student improvises *higher* on the keyboard)

More About Staff Reading

3rds (Skips) on the Staff

On the staff, the **interval of a 3rd (skip)** is from:

a LINE to the next LINE   or   a SPACE to the next SPACE

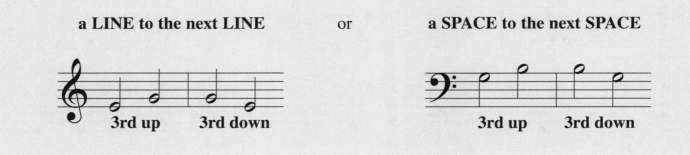

3rd up   3rd down   3rd up   3rd down

R.H. Warm-up with 3rds

Play this *line-to-line* 3rd with R.H. fingers **1-3**. Notice the dynamic marks.

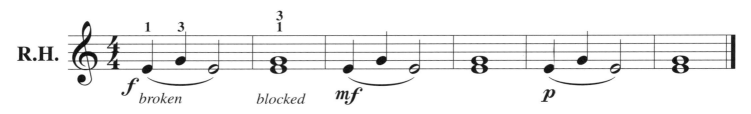

Repeat using R.H. fingers 2-4, then 3-5.

L.H. Warm-up with 3rds

Play this *space-to-space* 3rd with L.H. fingers **1-3**. Notice the dynamic marks.

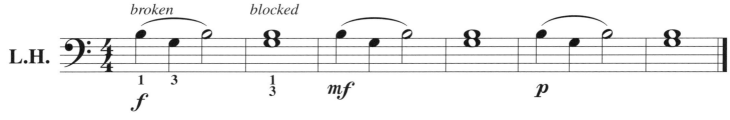

Repeat using L.H. fingers 2-4, then 3-5.

PLAY VIDEO

FF1302

Starlit Melody

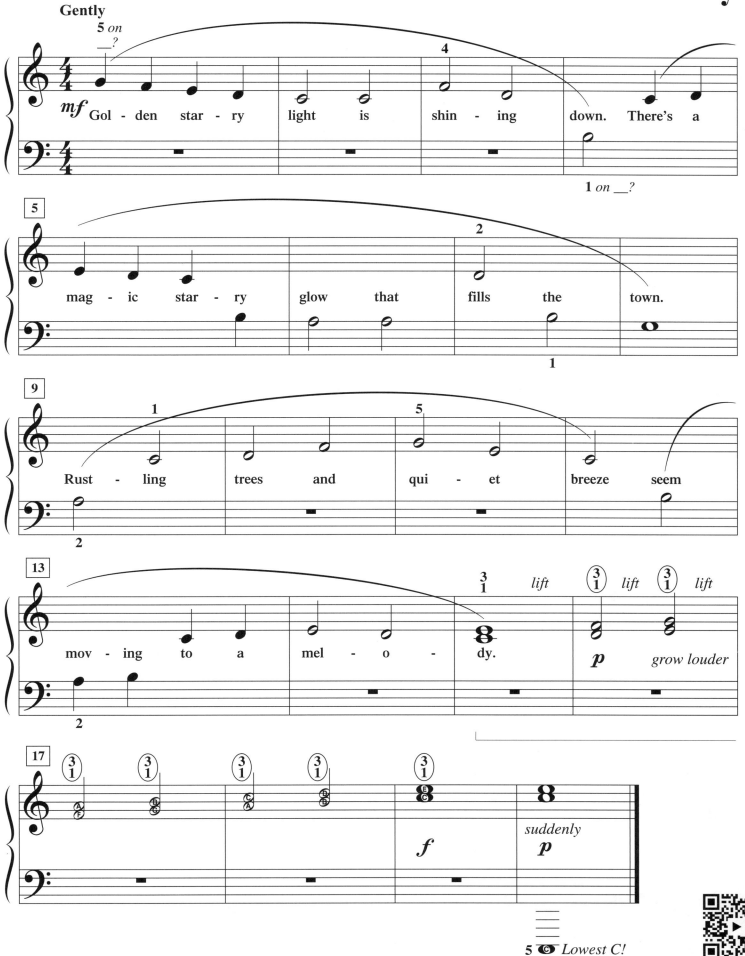

Quarter Rest

The quarter rest = 1 beat of *silence*

■ Tap (or clap) this rhythm example, counting aloud, **"1 - 2 - 3 - 4."**
Count, but **do not clap** (or play) for the quarter rest.

Eine Kleine Nachtmusik
(A Little Night Music)

Wolfgang Amadeus Mozart
(1756-1791, Austria)
arranged

Teacher Duet: (Student plays *1 octave higher*)

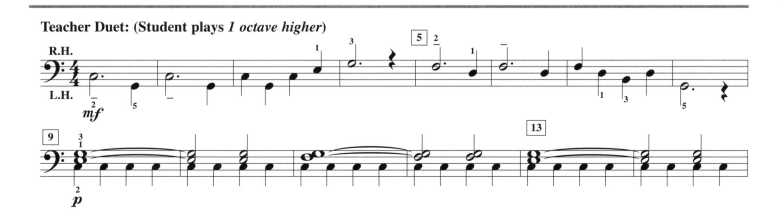

52

FF1302

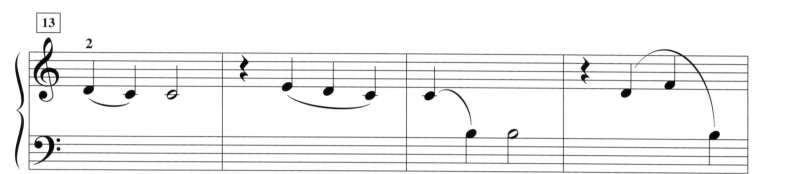

DISCOVERY Create two measures of $\frac{4}{4}$ rhythm and write them below. Include a **quarter rest**. Then tap (or clap) your rhythm.

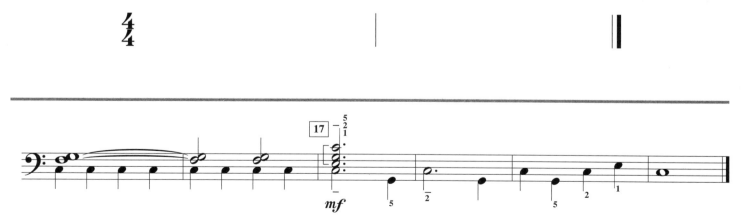

PLAY VIDEO

Melody and Harmony

- *melody* — the tune
- *harmony* — notes played with the melody to give a rich, fuller sound.

The interval of a **5th** (C up to G) is used to *harmonize* the melody in this piece.

Hand Placement

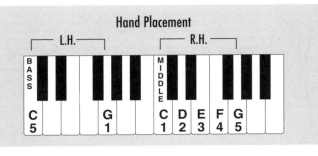

The Slavic composer Dvořák wrote this famous theme for his *Symphony No. 9, 'From the New World'*. "The New World" refers to America in the late 1800s.

New World Symphony Theme

Antonín Dvořák
(1841-1904, Bohemia)
arranged

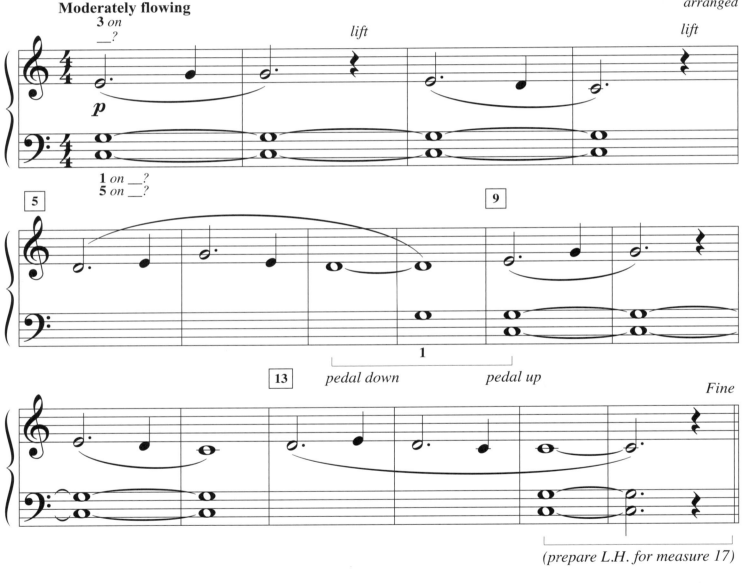

(*prepare L.H. for measure 17*)

Teacher Duet: (Student plays *1 octave higher* without pedal)

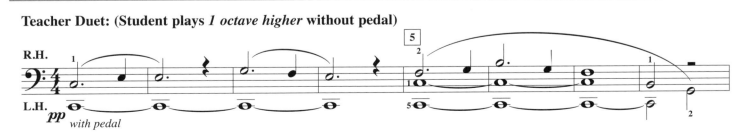

54

FF1302

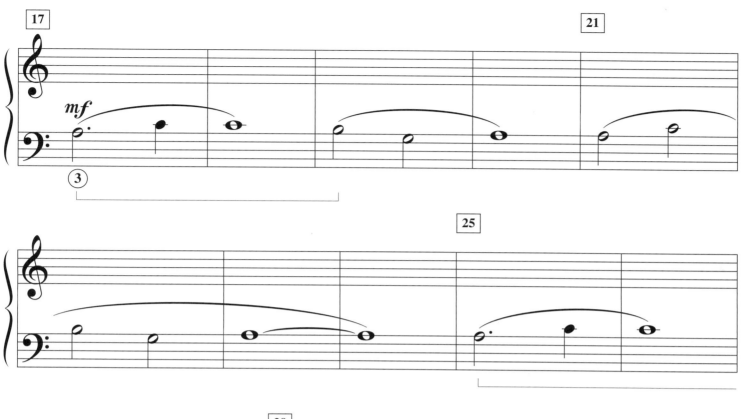

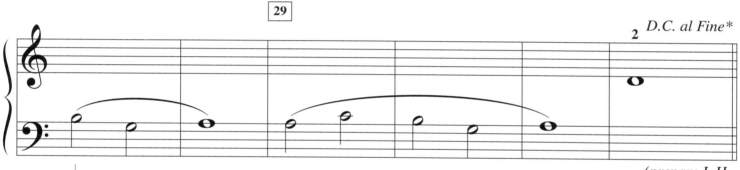

Da Capo al Fine

*D.C. al Fine means return to the beginning and play to *Fine*.
Da Capo (abbreviated D.C.) means from the beginning.
Fine (pronounced FEE-nay) means the end.

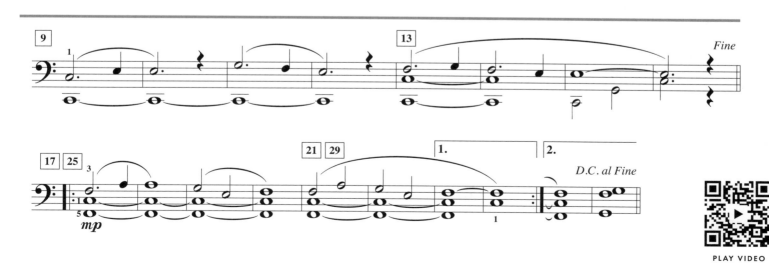

PLAY VIDEO

Playing a Chord

The word **chord** is derived from the Old French word *acorde*, meaning "to agree." Three or more tones played together form a chord.

The **C chord** is made of 3 tones built in *3rds* above C. A 3-note chord built in 3rds is also called a **triad**.

C chord (or triad)

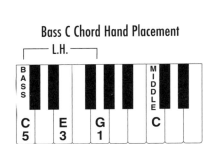

C Chord Warm-up

- On the closed key cover, "silently" play this L.H. exercise.
- On the piano, find the Bass C shown to the right.
- Practice *C Chord Warm-up* until it is secure.

Bass C Chord Hand Placement

Rather slowly

𝆑

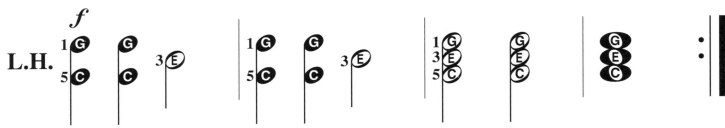

L.H.

- Now play *C Chord Warm-up* with your R.H. higher on the keyboard. Use **fingers 1–5**.

The C Chord (C - E - G) on the Bass Staff

- Notice that on the **bass staff** the top 3 spaces spell the **Bass C chord**. (bottom to top: **C-E-G**)

Note: Though these bass notes will be introduced formally on page 62, you may now use L.H. C chords with many of your early pieces.

Bass C Chord Hand Placement

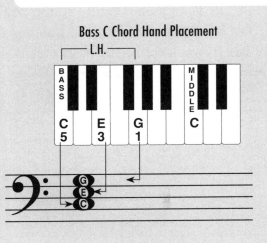

FF1302

Warm-up for Jingle Bells

■ In this piece, the interval of a **5th** and a **C chord** are used to harmonize the melody.

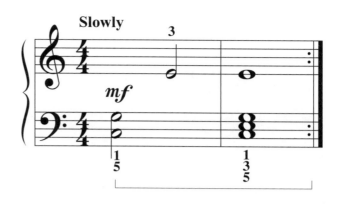

Jingle Bells

Words and Music by
J. Pierpont

Half and Whole Rests

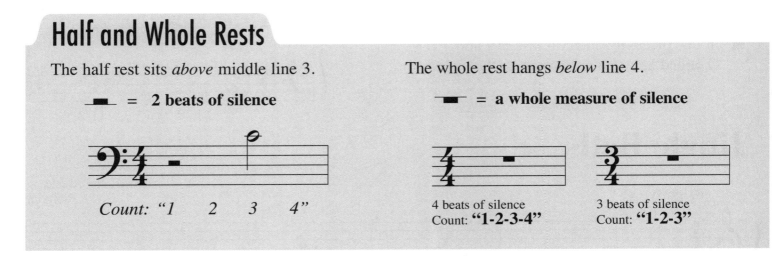

The half rest sits *above* middle line 3.

▬ = **2 beats of silence**

Count: "1   2   3   4"

The whole rest hangs *below* line 4.

▬ = **a whole measure of silence**

4 beats of silence
Count: **"1-2-3-4"**

3 beats of silence
Count: **"1-2-3"**

Rhythm Warm-up

■ Tap the rhythm below, counting aloud.

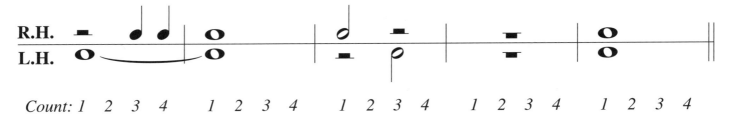

Count: 1 2 3 4   1 2 3 4   1 2 3 4   1 2 3 4   1 2 3 4

■ Identify each rest in *measures 1–8* as a
half rest or whole rest.

Royal Procession

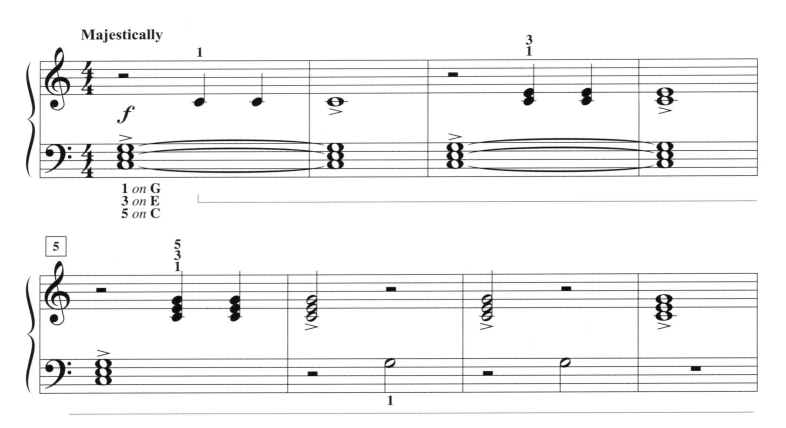

Majestically

f

1 *on* **G**
3 *on* **E**
5 *on* **C**

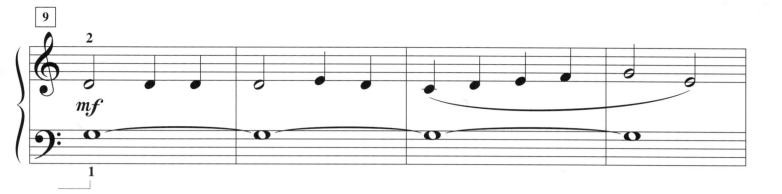

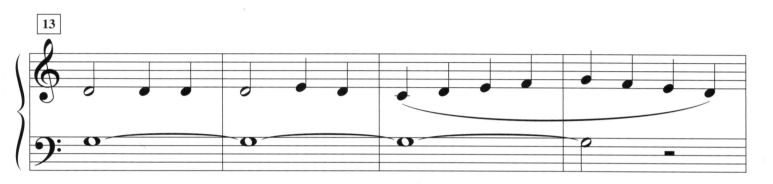

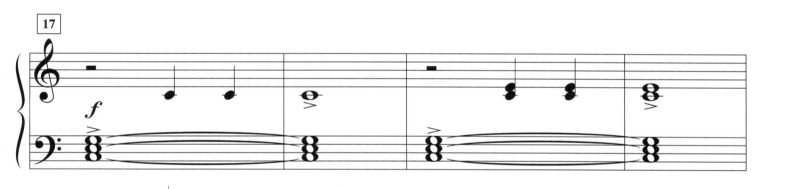

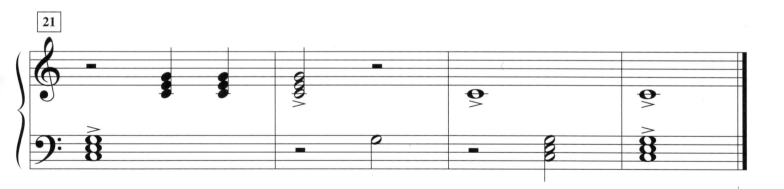

The form of this piece is **A B A¹**. Look for the section that is different. Mark it **B**. When section **A** returns at *measure 17*, compare it to *measures 1–8* to discover the difference in *measures 23–24*.

PLAY VIDEO

Technique Hints

■ Play the thumb on the side tip.

■ Keep your wrist flexible; however, do not let it sag as you play.

Study in Broken 3rds

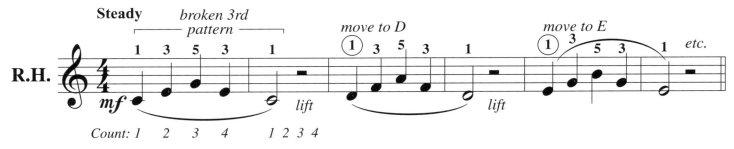

Continue these sequences up the white keys beginning on F, G, A, B, and C.

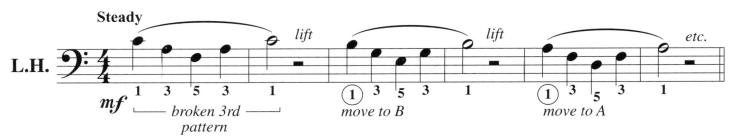

Continue these sequences down the white keys beginning on G, F, E, D, and C.

Rhythm Study

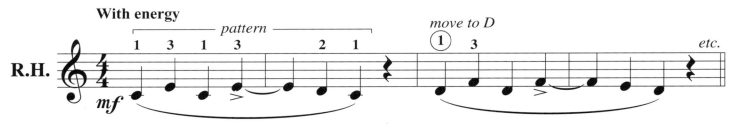

Continue these sequences up the white keys beginning on E, F, G, A, B, and C.

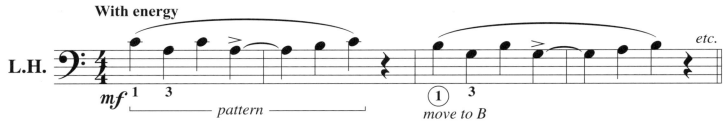

Continue these sequences down the white keys beginning on A, G, F, E, D, and C.

PLAY VIDEO

Review of 3rds (See page 50)

On the staff, the **interval of a 3rd** (skip) is from:

a LINE to the next LINE   or a   SPACE to the next SPACE

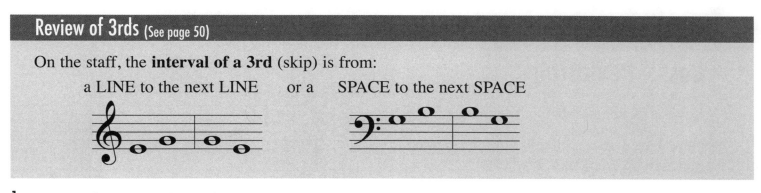

1. Draw a **3rd up** or **down** from each note below. Use whole notes.
   Then name both notes in the blanks.

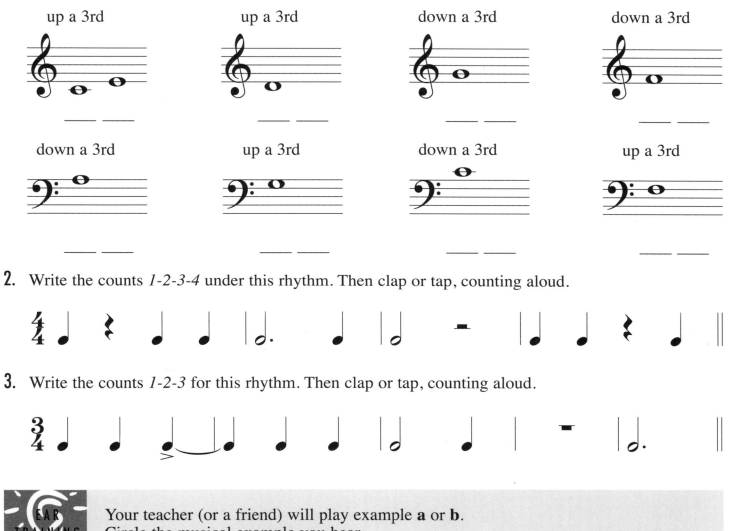

up a 3rd   up a 3rd   down a 3rd   down a 3rd

down a 3rd   up a 3rd   down a 3rd   up a 3rd

2. Write the counts *1-2-3-4* under this rhythm. Then clap or tap, counting aloud.

3. Write the counts *1-2-3* for this rhythm. Then clap or tap, counting aloud.

EAR TRAINING

Your teacher (or a friend) will play example **a** or **b**.
Circle the musical example you hear.

1a.   2a.   3a.

or   or   or

1b.   2b.   3b.

More Bass Clef Note Reading

Bass C Pentascale

Review: A pentascale is a five-note scale.

New: Familiarize yourself with these notes that step up from **Bass C**.

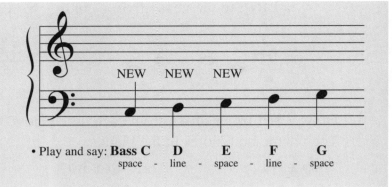

NEW   NEW   NEW

• Play and say: **Bass C**   **D**   **E**   **F**   **G**
space - line - space - line - space

Rules for Stems

Notice the stem on **Bass C** goes *up*. The stems on **Bass D**, **E**, **F**, and **G** go *down*.

Notes *below* the middle line
(line 3) have UP stems.

Notes *on or above* line 3
have DOWN stems.

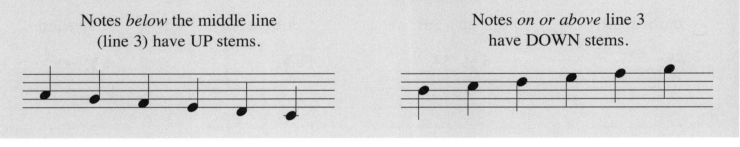

Bass Clef Melodies

■ First tap (or clap) each melody. Count aloud.

■ Play each melody s-l-o-w-l-y, then at a moderate tempo.

■ Notice each melody begins on a *different* note of the **Bass C Pentascale**.

Give My Regards to Broadway   George M. Cohan

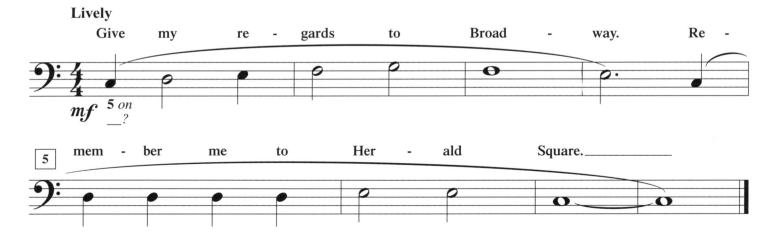

Rise and Shine

Traditional spiritual

Cheerfully

Rise___ and shine___ and give God the glo - ry, glo - ry.

f **4** *on* ___?

Ode to Joy

Ludwig van Beethoven

Moderately

mp **3** *on* ___?

5

All Through the Night

Traditional lullaby

Gently

Sleep, my child and peace at - tend thee, all through the night._____

p **2** *on* ___?

Lightly Row

Traditional

Brightly

mf **1** *on* ___?

5

PLAY VIDEO

Staccato

Staccato sounds are crisp and detached. To play *staccato*, quickly bring the finger off the key. The staccato mark is a small dot placed above or below the note.

Warm-ups

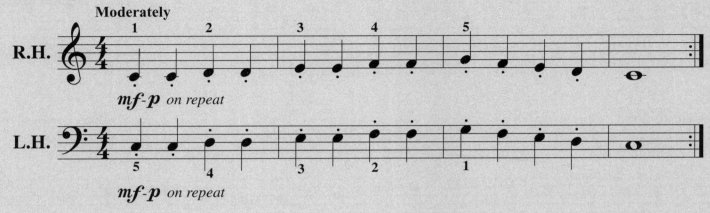

The Octave

From *Middle C* to *Bass C* is the distance of 8 white keys and spans 8 letter names: C-B-A-G-F-E-D-C. This is the interval of an **octave**.

Theme from the
"Surprise" Symphony

Franz Joseph Haydn
(1732–1809, Austria)
arranged

■ This piece begins with the hands playing an octave apart.

A circled finger number alerts ① you to a change of hand placement.

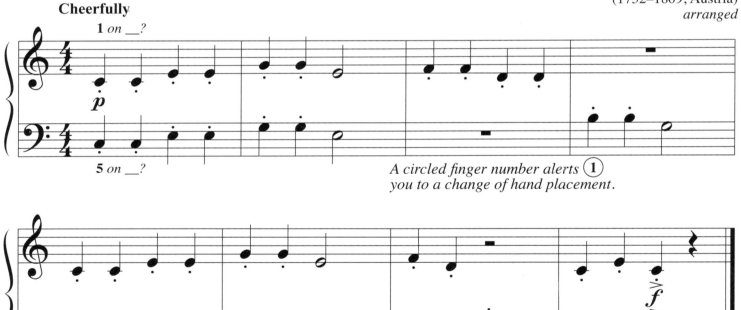

PLAY VIDEO

64

FF1302

Hungarian Dance

Johannes Brahms
(1833-1897, Germany)
arranged

Repeat Signs
Play the section within
the repeat signs again.

Teacher Duet: (Student plays *1 octave higher*)

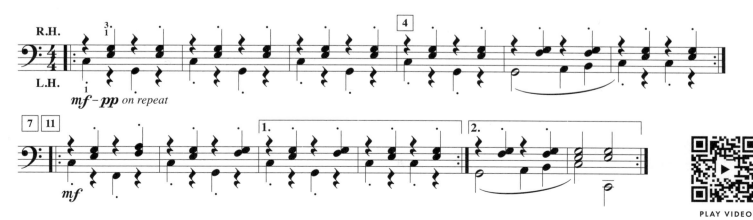

PLAY VIDEO

> ### *rit.* - ritardando
>
> This means a gradual slowing of the music.
> *Ritardando* is often shortened to *ritard.* or *rit.*

Shepherd's Song
(From the Sixth Symphony)

Ludwig van Beethoven
(1770–1827, Germany)
arranged

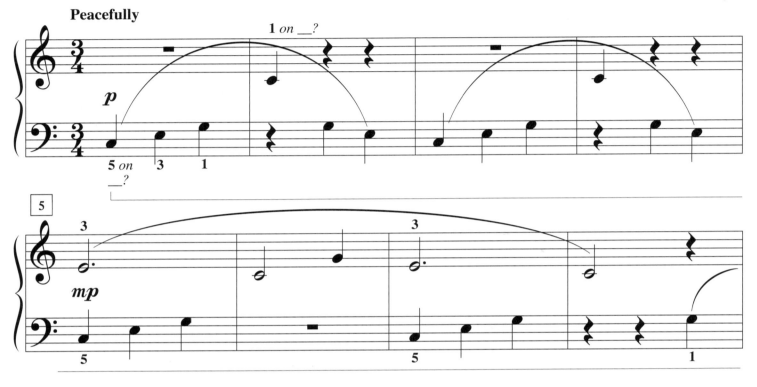

Teacher Duet: (Student plays *1 octave higher*)

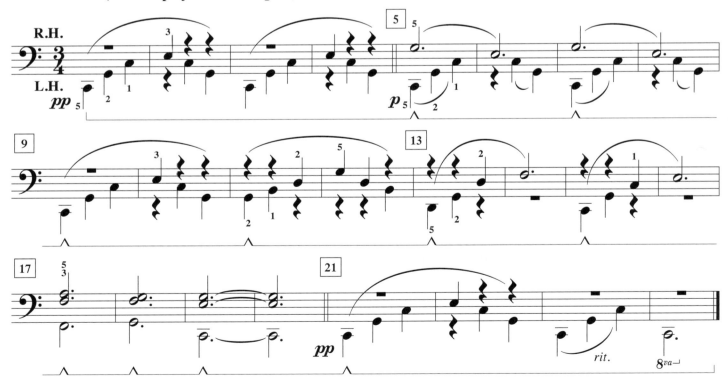

FF1302

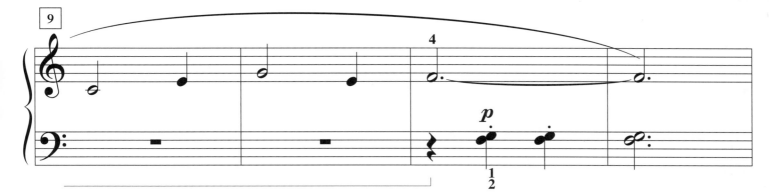

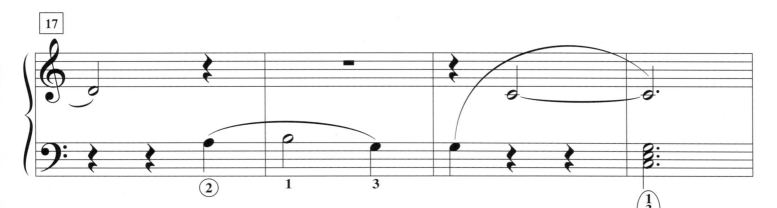

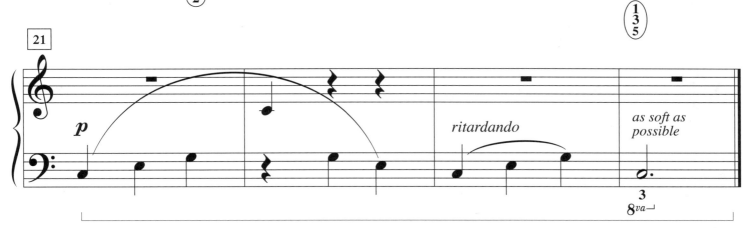

The beats of a 3/4 time signature have this feeling: (*circle one*)

strong-weak-strong   strong-weak-weak   strong-strong-weak

PLAY VIDEO

Parallel Promenade

> **Parallel Motion:** Hands-together playing with the notes moving in the SAME direction.

■ Practice both exercises at slow, medium, and faster *tempi* (plural of tempo).

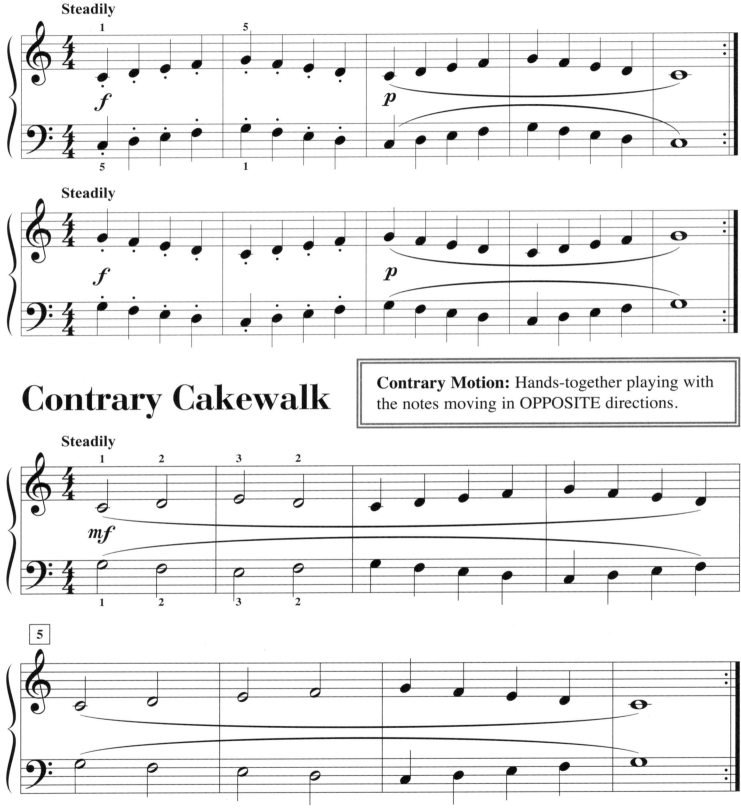

Contrary Cakewalk

> **Contrary Motion:** Hands-together playing with the notes moving in OPPOSITE directions.

PLAY VIDEO

Extra Practice: Repeat both exercises with the R.H. 1 octave HIGHER.
Repeat both exercises with the L.H. 1 octave LOWER.

FF1302

1. Use the example below to help you write the five notes of the **Bass C Pentascale**.
   Remember, the stem on **Bass C** goes *up* and to the *right*.
   The stems on **Bass D E F** and **G** go *down* and to the *left*. (See p. 62)

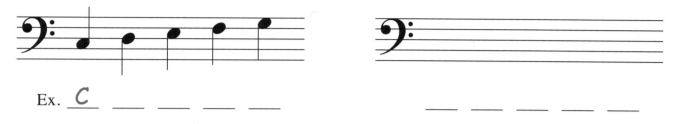

Ex. C ___ ___ ___ ___   ___ ___ ___ ___ ___

2. Lightly shade the **Bass C space** for each staff below. Then, using quarter notes, draw the notes
   specified that are in the **Bass C Pentascale**. Add stems correctly on each note.

    C D E   D F E   C E G   G F D

Ex.

3. ## Staccato Improvisation

   ◼ Ask a friend or your teacher to play the duet part below. First, listen and feel the beat.

   ◼ When you are ready, improvise a *staccato* melody using the **Bass C Pentascale** notes
   (C-D-E-F-G) *in any order*. End on Bass C for a final conclusion.

Teacher Duet: (Student improvises *using Bass C-D-E-F-G*)

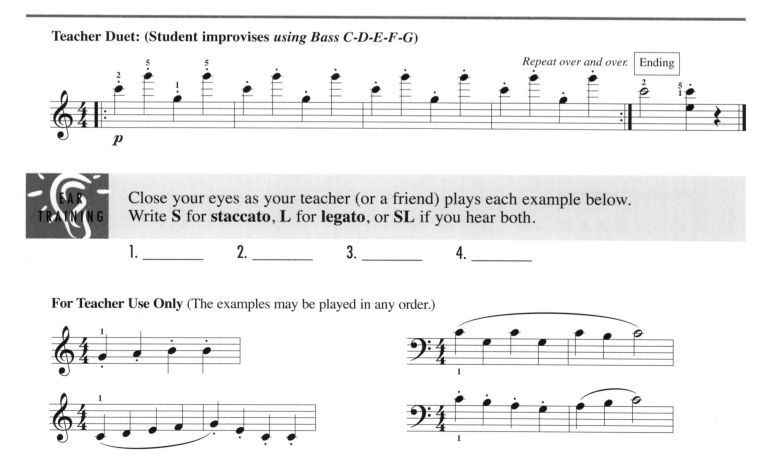

Repeat over and over. | Ending

EAR TRAINING — Close your eyes as your teacher (or a friend) plays each example below.
Write **S** for **staccato**, **L** for **legato**, or **SL** if you hear both.

1. _____ 2. _____ 3. _____ 4. _____

For Teacher Use Only (The examples may be played in any order.)

Eighth (8th) Notes

Eighth Notes

A single eighth note has a *flag*.

flag

2 eighth notes = 1 quarter note

■ Two (or more) eighth notes are connected by a beam.

beam

run - ning   walk

■ Think of quarter notes as *walking* notes and eighth (8th) notes as *running* notes.

Counting Eighth Notes

For rhythms with **eighth notes**, each beat is *divided* into two equal parts. In the rhythms below, each eighth note receives one-half beat.

1   and   2   and
1   +   2   +

■ Tap (or clap) the rhythms below while counting aloud.

■ Count the 8th note between the beats using the word "and" (written "+").

■ Choose any key on the piano and play each rhythm, counting aloud.

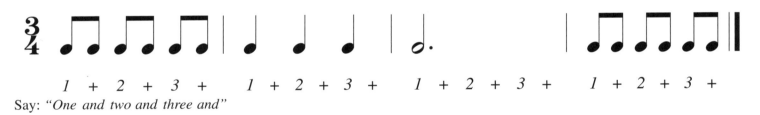

1 + 2 + 3 +   1 + 2 + 3 +   1 + 2 + 3 +   1 + 2 + 3 +

Say: *"One and two and three and"*

Notice four eighth notes are often beamed together.

1 + 2 + 3 + 4 +   1 + 2 + 3 + 4 +   1 + 2 + 3 + 4 +   1 + 2 + 3 + 4 +

 Clap each rhythm with the metronome ticking at :   ♩ = 72   ♩ = 88   ♩ = 104

PLAY VIDEO

FF1302

mezzo piano (*mp*) means moderately soft	A **minuet** is a stately dance in ¾ time.

■ Rhythm Check: Are your eighth notes flowing gently, with a steady, even rhythm?

French Minuet

Jean-Philippe Rameau
(1683–1764, France)
arranged

Flowing smoothly, rather slowly

DISCOVERY	This piece uses two intervals: ___ and ___. Circle the **3rds**. (There are 8.)	 PLAY VIDEO

Teacher Duet: (Student plays *1 octave higher*)

Crescendo and Diminuendo

crescendo (*cresc.*)
means play gradually louder
(pronounced "kreh-SHEN-doh").

diminuendo (*dim.*)
means play gradually softer
(pronounced "di-min-u-EN-doh").

This symbol 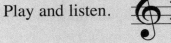 is also called *decrescendo*
(day-kreh-SHEN-doh).

Play and listen.

Play and listen.

Phrase

A **phrase** is a musical idea or "sentence."

A phrase is often shown in the music with a long slur,
also called a *phrase mark*.

■ Notice the long eight-measure phrases in *Morning*.
  "Shape" each phrase with a ⟨ and ⟩ as marked.

Morning
(from *Peer Gynt Suite No. 1*)

Edvard Grieg
(1843-1907, Norway)
arranged

FF1302

DISCOVERY Transpose the melody only in *measures 9–16* with your R.H. beginning on D.
Hint: Read by **2nds** and **3rds**.

Teacher Duet: (Student plays *1 octave higher,* without pedal)

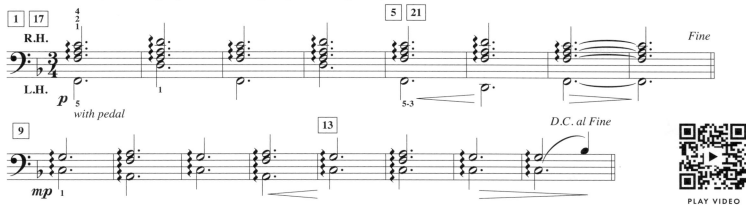

PLAY VIDEO

Upbeat (or Pick-up Note)

The first beat of any complete measure is referred to as the *downbeat*. Upbeat(s) or pick-up note(s) lead into the first full measure. This piece begins on *beat 4* with **two eighth notes** on the upbeat (*4 and*).

If a piece begins with an upbeat, the last measure is often incomplete. The combined beats of the incomplete first and last measures will equal one full measure.

Taps

U.S. Army Bugle Call

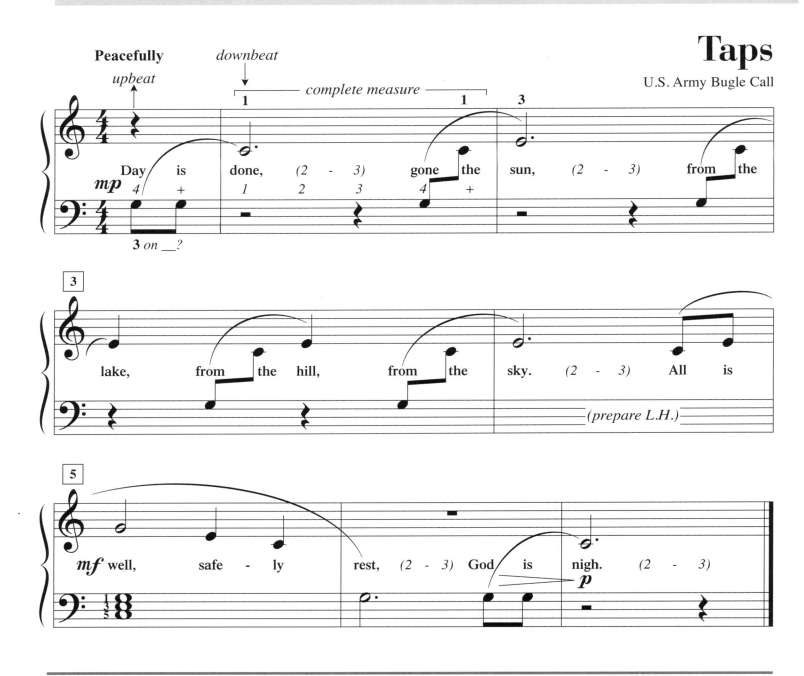

Teacher Duet: (Student plays *1 octave higher*)

PLAY VIDEO

FF1302

Fermata 𝄐 (Pronounced fer-MAH-tah)
Hold this note longer than usual.

This piece begins on *beat 3* with two eighth notes on the upbeat (*3 and*).

Happy Birthday

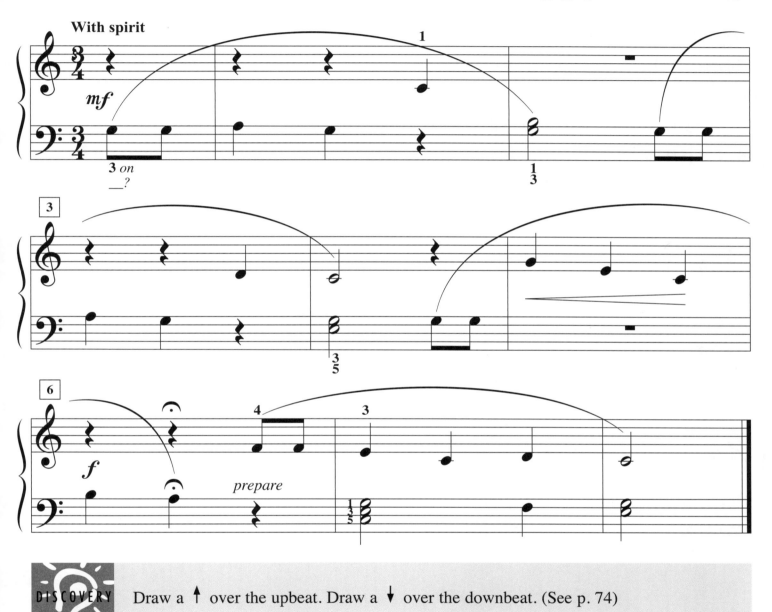

DISCOVERY   Draw a ↑ over the upbeat. Draw a ↓ over the downbeat. (See p. 74)

Teacher Duet: (Student plays *1 octave higher*)

PLAY VIDEO

FF1302

The C Major Chord: Root - 3rd - 5th

The 3 tones of the C major chord (or C major triad) build up in **3rds** from C.

■ G is the 5th
■ E is the 3rd
■ C is the root

This folk song is composed only of C **chord tones**.

■ In each blank, write **blocked** or **broken** to describe the chord.

■ Write the 3 letter names used in this piece. _____, _____, _____

■ The R.H. begins on the **3rd** of the C chord in 3 measures: ___, ___, and ___.

English Folk Song

Traditional

Cheerfully

mf

 FF1302

The Csus4 Chord

"Sus4" is short for "suspended 4th."

The **sus4 chord** uses the *4th* note (F) in place of the *3rd* note (E) to give a suspended feeling to this chord.

The **Csus4** chord usually resolves to the **C chord**, for a feeling of peaceful resolution.

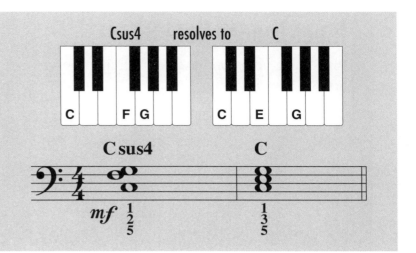

Chord symbol

The letter name of a chord, written *above* the treble staff, indicates the harmony.

A **gavotte** is a lively French dance in $\frac{4}{4}$ time. It usually begins with two upbeats.

Gavotte

George Frideric Handel
(1685–1759, Germany)
arranged

Inner Ledger Note B

Play these notes on the piano, saying the
note names aloud.

C   B = C   B

R.H. Warm-ups

1. For this warm-up, *extend* the thumb (thumb extension) to play **ledger note B**.

2. Now cross finger 2 *over* the thumb to play **ledger note B**.

crosses over

Teacher Duet for *Simple Gifts*, page 79: (Student plays *1 octave higher*)

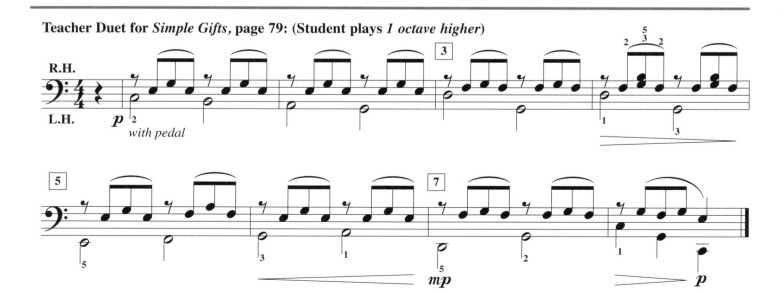

FF1302

Simple Gifts

Traditional Shaker melody
arranged

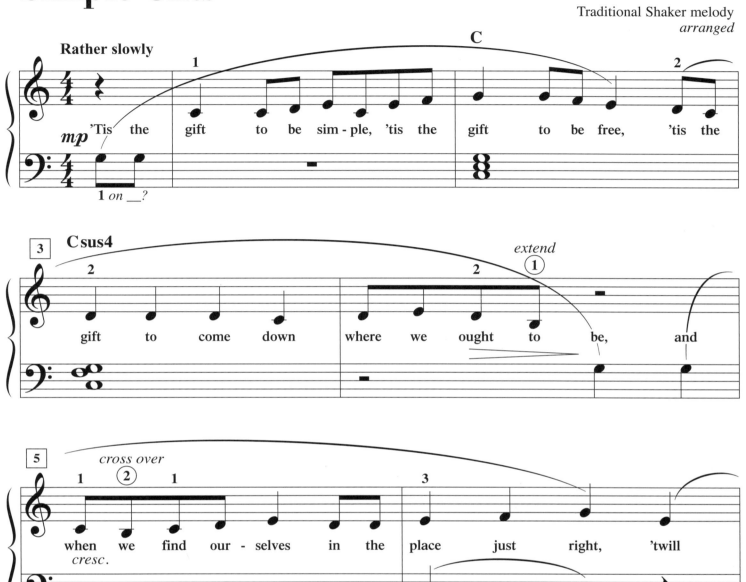

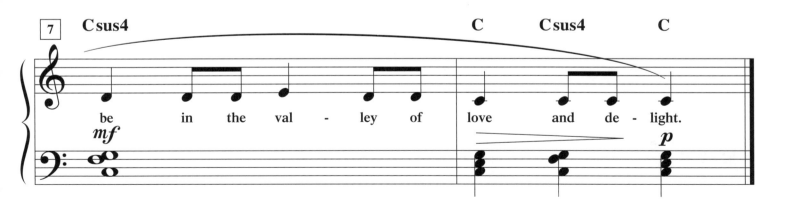

 DISCOVERY   On what beat does the opening *upbeat* occur?

PLAY VIDEO

Review of Tempo

Tempo is the speed of the beat. (Plural is *tempi*.)

■ Tap each Rhythm Drill at a moderate tempo.

■ Practice on the piano at slow, moderate, and fast *tempi*.

Rhythm Drills

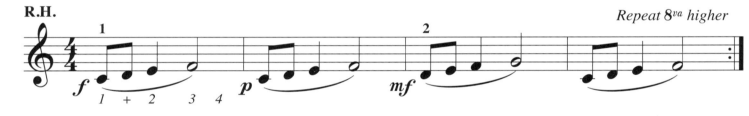

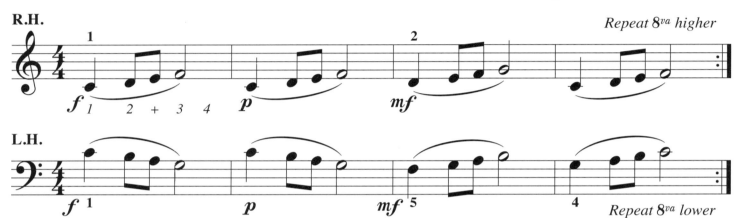

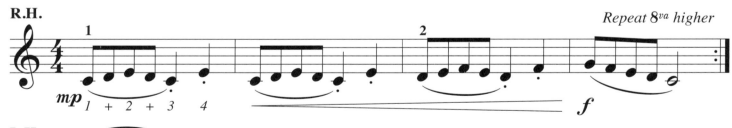

PLAY VIDEO

FF1302

Review of 8th Notes (See page 70)

1. Draw *one note* to equal the 8th notes below.

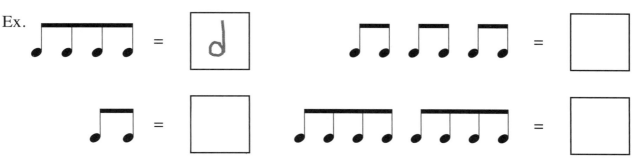

2. Each measure below is incomplete. Complete each measure using **8th notes** (♫ or ♫♫).
   Then play the rhythms on any white key at a moderate tempo.

3. Write **1 + 2 + 3 + 4 +** (*1 and 2 and 3 and 4 and*) under this melody.
   Then sightread the music. Set a steady beat by counting one free measure before starting.

   Write **1 + 2 + 3 +** for this melody. Then sightread the music, counting as you play.

4. Identify each example as a **C chord** or **Csus4 chord**. Then play each.

   Ex. Csus4

Treble Space Notes: F-A-C-E

F-A-C-E the Spaces

The space notes on the treble staff spell the word **F A C E**.

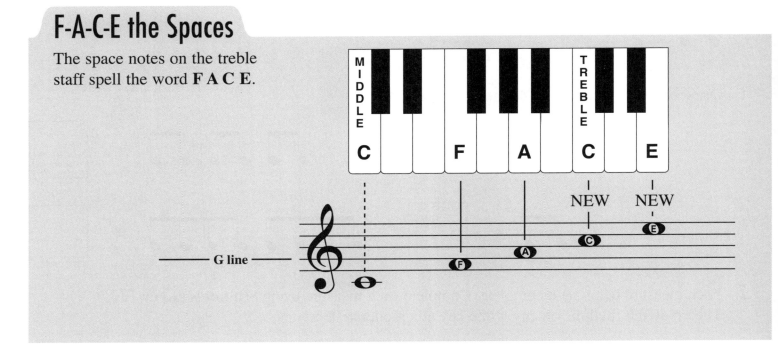

Space Note Warm-up

■ Starting with the F above Middle C, **play** and **say** the treble space notes F-A-C-E, going up and going down. Use R.H. finger 2.

■ Are you playing **2nds** or **3rds**?

Moon on the Water

■ Before playing, write the name of each note in the blank for *measures 1–4*.

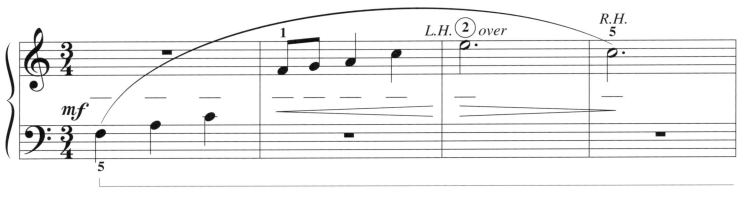

Teacher Duet: (Student plays *1 octave higher*, without pedal)

FF1302

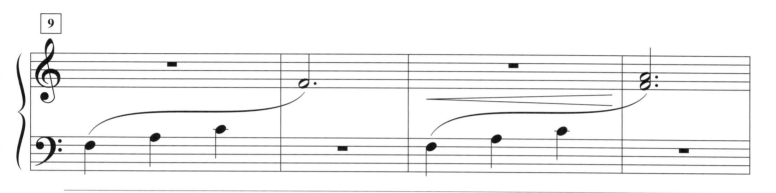

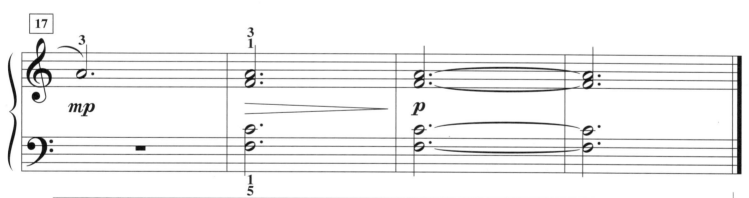

 DISCOVERY Transpose *Moon on the Water* to the notes of the **C pentascale**.

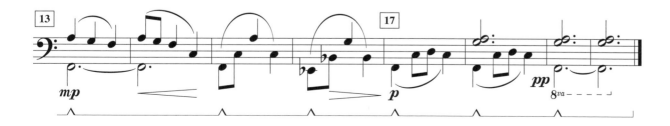

PLAY VIDEO

FF1302

83

This beautiful, old melody dates back over 500 years. It has had many different words written through the centuries, including an Italian song, Spanish hymn, Polish and Swedish folk song, and the Israeli national anthem, among others.

500-Year-Old Melody

Hatikvah, based on a 16th century Italian melody

Teacher Duet: (Student plays *1 octave higher*)

84

FF1302

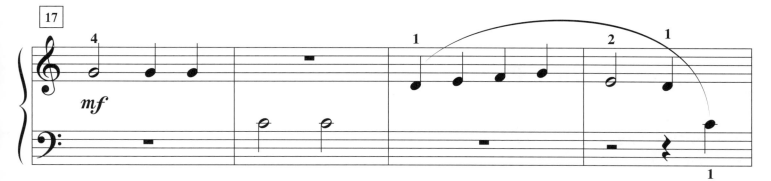

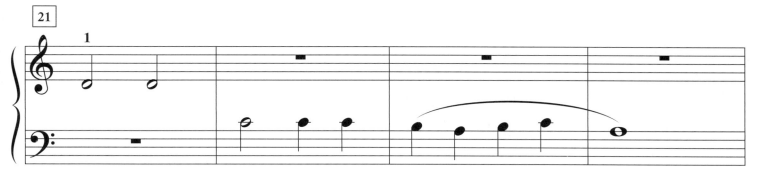

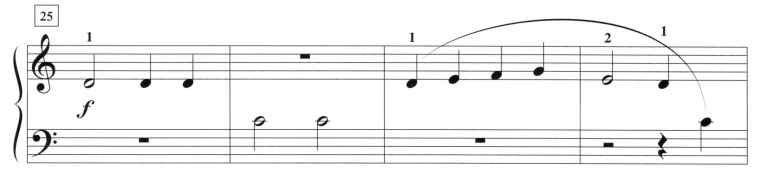

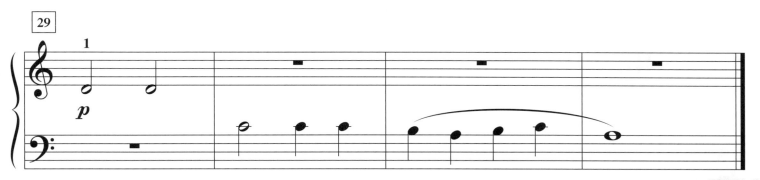

DISCOVERY Can you name and define each **dynamic mark** in this piece?

PLAY VIDEO

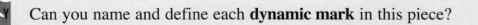

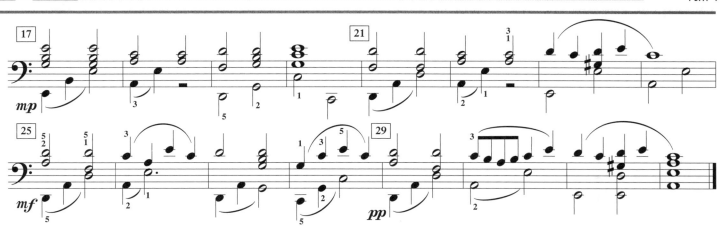

Playing the F Major Chord

The **F major chord** (or **F major triad**)
is made of 3 tones built in *3rds* above F.

F major chord

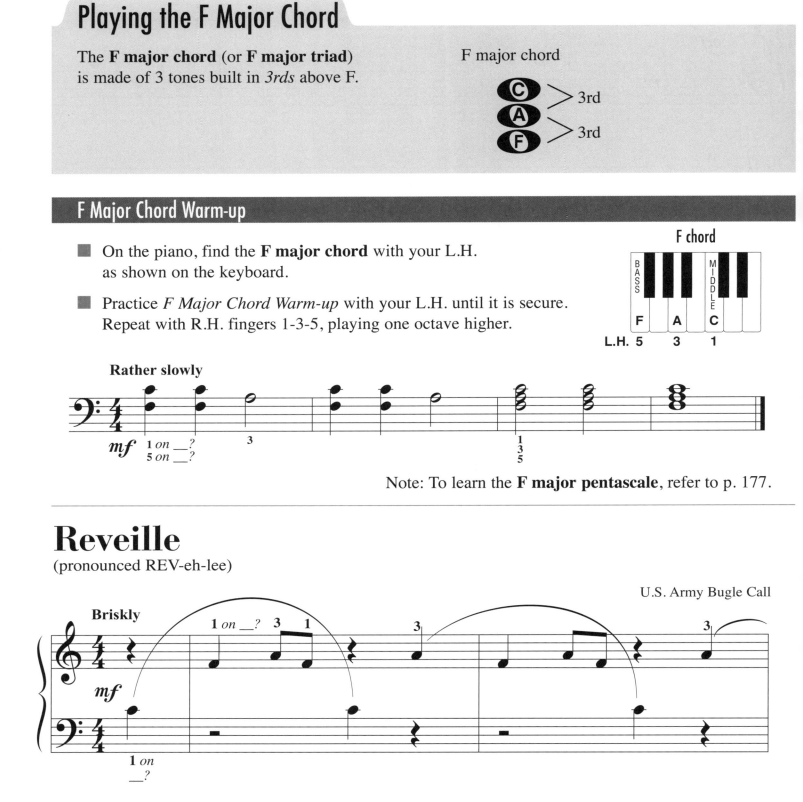

F Major Chord Warm-up

- On the piano, find the **F major chord** with your L.H.
  as shown on the keyboard.

- Practice *F Major Chord Warm-up* with your L.H. until it is secure.
  Repeat with R.H. fingers 1-3-5, playing one octave higher.

F chord

Rather slowly

mf **1** *on* __?
      5 *on* __?   3

Note: To learn the **F major pentascale**, refer to p. 177.

Reveille
(pronounced REV-eh-lee)

U.S. Army Bugle Call

Briskly

mf

1 *on*
__?

Teacher Duet: (Student plays *1 octave higher*)

R.H.

L.H. mf

f

86   FF1302

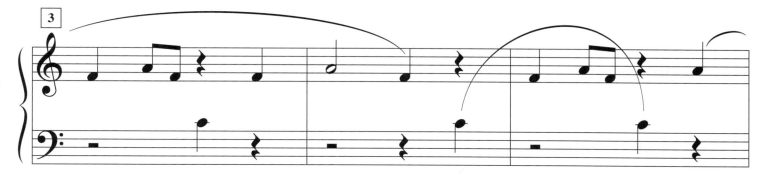

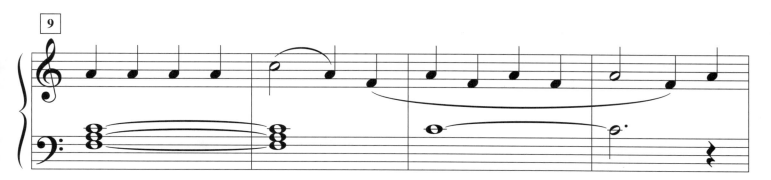

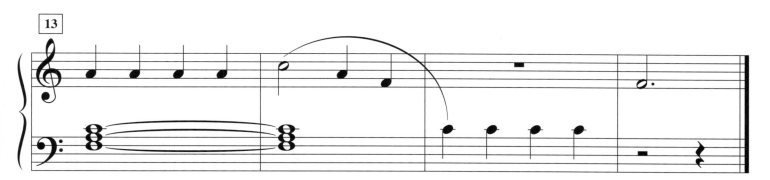

DISCOVERY Transpose *Reveille* to the notes of the **C pentascale**. (L.H. begins on **G**; R.H. begins on **C**). Observe the finger numbers, read the intervals, and use your ear.

PLAY VIDEO

Arpeggio

Arpeggio (pronounced "ar-PEJ-ee-oh") comes from the Italian word for "harp." To play an arpeggio, play the **notes of a chord** one after another, going up or down the keyboard.

Cross-Hand Arpeggios

■ Practice these **cross-hand arpeggios** until you can play them smoothly and easily.

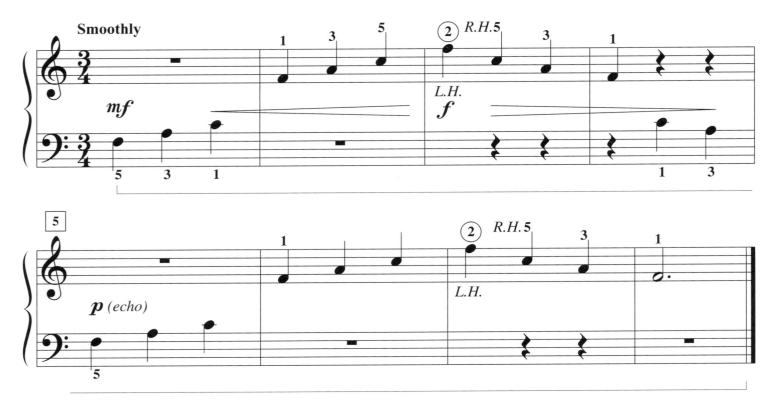

■ Continue *Cross-Hand Arpeggios* using these hand positions:

Down a 2nd: **beginning on E**

Down a 2nd: **beginning on D**

Down a 2nd: **beginning on C**

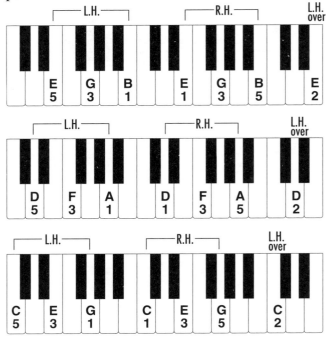

PLAY VIDEO

FF1302

1. Name each space note below. Then play each with your R.H., using the fingering given.

---

2. Write the counts under examples **a** and **b**. Tap or clap, counting aloud. Then sightread.

EAR TRAINING

Your teacher (or a friend) will play the given note and then another note a 3rd up or 3rd down. Close your eyes and listen. Draw a note a 3rd up or down from the given note. Play and name both notes.

a.   b.   c.   d.

Improvisation with Treble Spaces F-A-C-E

■ Ask your teacher or a friend to play the duet below. First, *listen* and feel the beat.

■ When you are ready, improvise a R.H. melody using treble spaces F-A-C-E in any order.

R.H. Placement

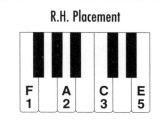

F A C E
1 2 3 5

Teacher Duet: (Student improvises *higher* on the keyboard.)

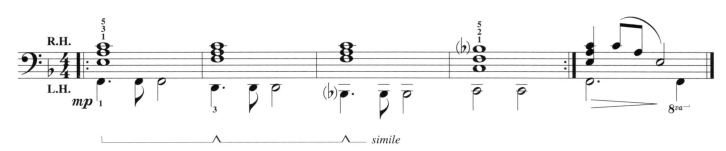

Treble C Pentascale

Playing Treble C-D-E-F-G

Learn these notes that step up by 2nds from **Treble C**. (You already know the circled notes.)

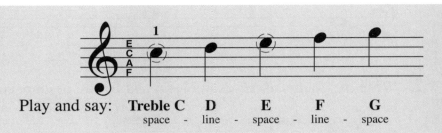

Play and say: **Treble C**   **D**   **E**   **F**   **G**
space - line - space - line - space

Learn and play this piece by:

- reading *2nds*, *3rds*, and *repeated notes*
- recognizing note names, **Treble C D E F G**
- practicing slowly, as you count aloud.

May Dance

Cheerfully

Count: 1 and 2 and 3 and | 1 and 2 and 3 and | 1 and 2 and 3 and | etc.

1 on __?

Teacher Duet: (Student plays *1 octave higher*)

mp - pp on repeat

PLAY VIDEO

FF1302

When the Saints Go Marching In

Traditional

Teacher Duet: (Student plays *1 octave higher*)

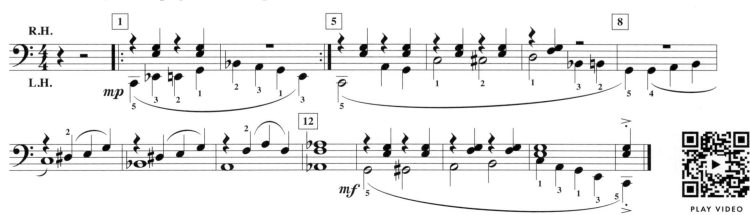

PLAY VIDEO

Review of *rit.* - ritardando (See page 66)

This means a gradual slowing of the music. *Ritardando* is often shortened to *ritard.* or *rit.*

■ Notice that in *measure 25* the R.H. shifts higher to Treble C.

African Celebration

Traditional African melody

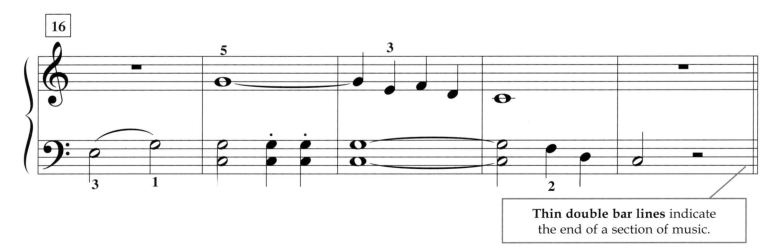

Thin double bar lines indicate the end of a section of music.

FF1302

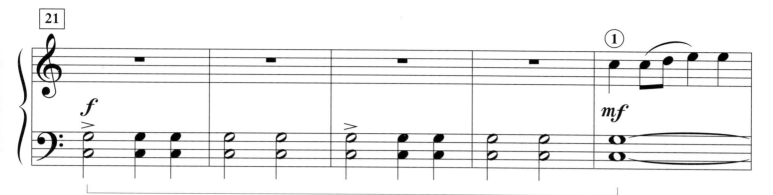

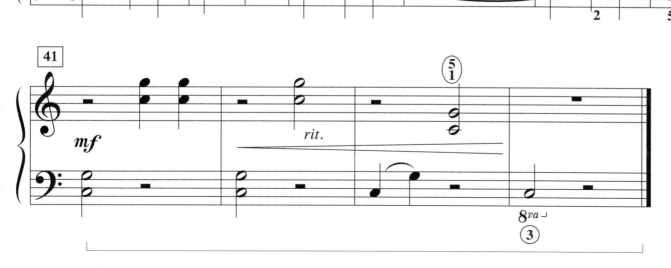

PLAY VIDEO

Imitative Study

■ Notice that the R.H. *imitates* each L.H. musical pattern. Play on firm fingertips, keeping the eighth notes very steady.

Imitation

Imitation is the immediate repetition of a musical idea played by the other hand.

■ Turn back to p. 91 and find the imitation in that piece.

PLAY VIDEO

FF1302

1. Draw the notes of three **C Pentascales** in different locations on the grand staff.
   Use whole notes. Write the note names in the blanks.

Begin on **Bass** C   Begin on **Middle** C   Begin on **Treble** C

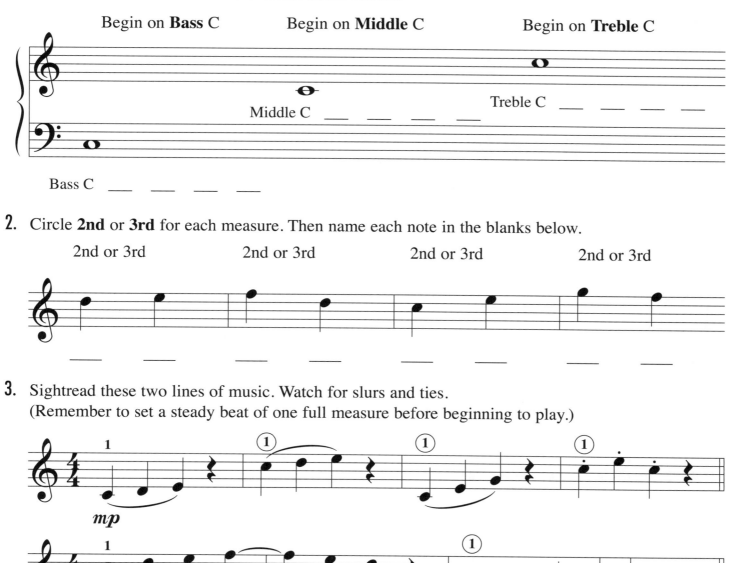

Middle C __ __ __ __

Treble C __ __ __ __

Bass C __ __ __ __

2. Circle **2nd** or **3rd** for each measure. Then name each note in the blanks below.

2nd or 3rd   2nd or 3rd   2nd or 3rd   2nd or 3rd

___ ___   ___ ___   ___ ___   ___ ___

3. Sightread these two lines of music. Watch for slurs and ties.
   (Remember to set a steady beat of one full measure before beginning to play.)

mp

mf

EAR TRAINING Listen as your teacher plays intervals of a **2nd** or **3rd** *broken*, then *blocked*. Circle 2nd or 3rd below.

a. 2nd   **b.** 2nd   **c.** 2nd   **d.** 2nd   **e.** 2nd

   3rd   3rd   3rd   3rd   3rd

For Teacher Use Only (The examples may be played in any order and repeated several times.)

G Pentascales in 3 Locations

Playing G-A-B-C-D on the Grand Staff

The 5 notes of the **G pentascale** are **G A B C D**.

■ Find and play these G pentascales on the piano. Say the letter names aloud.

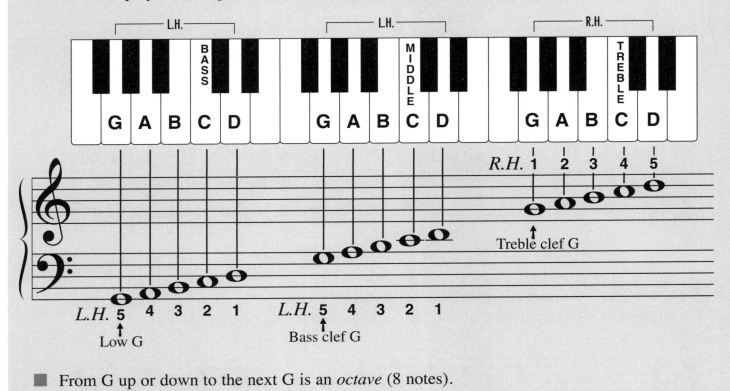

■ From G up or down to the next G is an *octave* (8 notes).

■ Practice *Octave Warm-up* to help you memorize the location of these 3 G's on the piano.

Octave Warm-up

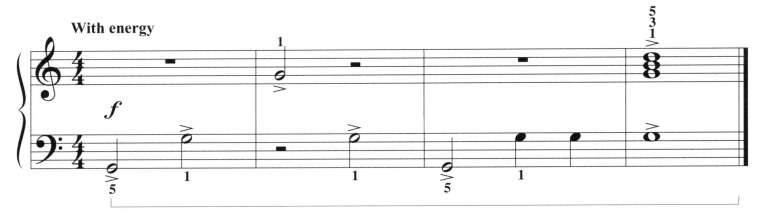

With energy

PLAY VIDEO

FF1302

G Pentascale Warm-ups

Treble Clef G Warm-up

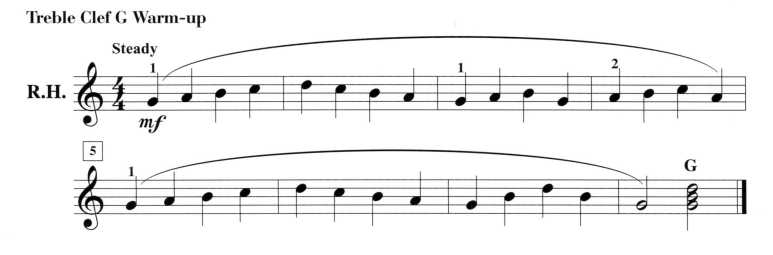

Bass Clef G Warm-up

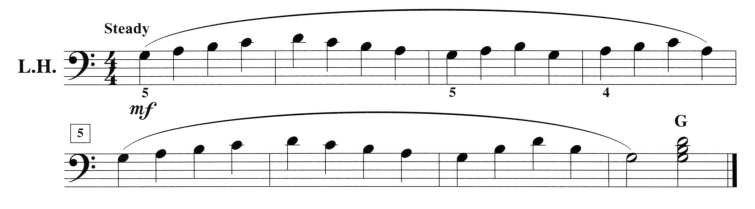

Low G Warm-up

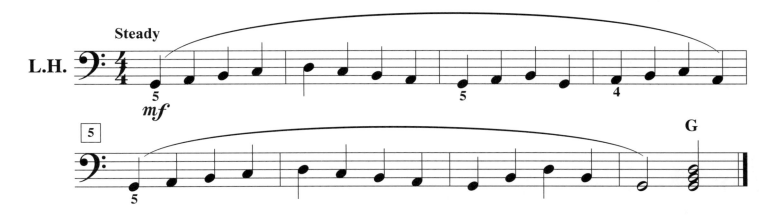

PLAY VIDEO

Italian Tempo Marks

Remember, *tempo* means the speed of the music (fast, slow, etc.). The tempo mark is located at the beginning of a piece, just above the time signature. Italian words are commonly used as tempo marks.

←——— **SLOWER** ———   ——— **FASTER** ———→

Andante	**Moderato**	**Allegro**
(ahn-DAHN-tay)	(mod-eh-RAH-toh)	(ah-LEH-groh)
"walking speed"	moderately	fast and lively

A **musette** is a lively piece imitating the bagpipe.

Musette

composer unknown
from the Anna Magdalena Bach Notebook
adapted

■ Name the pentascale used below: _____

![DISCOVERY] Transpose *Musette* to the notes of the **C pentascale**.
For additional pentascales, see page 176.

PLAY VIDEO

FF1302

Old Irish Blessing

■ Name the pentascale used below: _____

Traditional Words

DISCOVERY Transpose *Old Irish Blessing* to the notes of the **C pentascale**.
For additional pentascales, see page 176.

PLAY VIDEO

The G and Gsus4 Chords

L.H. Warm-up

Theme by Mozart*

Key of G Major

Wolfgang Amadeus Mozart
(1756-1791, Austria)
arranged

Teacher Duet: (Student plays *1 octave higher*)

*From *Sonata in A Major*, K. 331

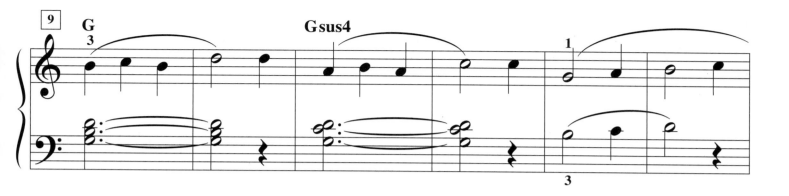

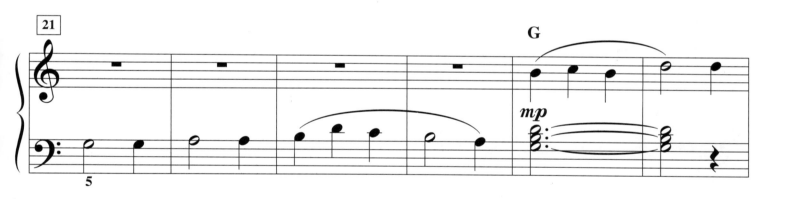

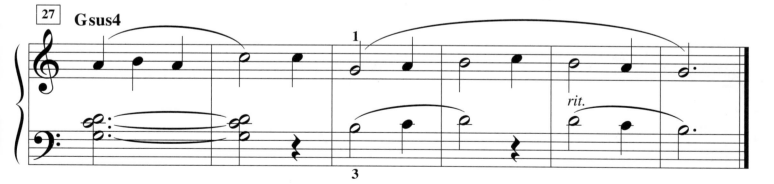

 **DISCOVERY** How many beats does each *whole rest* receive in this piece?

PLAY VIDEO

■ Tap the rhythm on the closed keyboard cover or your lap, counting aloud, **"1-2-3-4, 1 + 2 + 3 + 4 +,"** etc.

■ Name the pentascale used below: _____

■ Then play, counting aloud.

Finger Fanfare

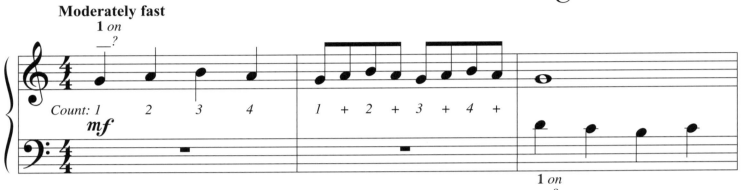

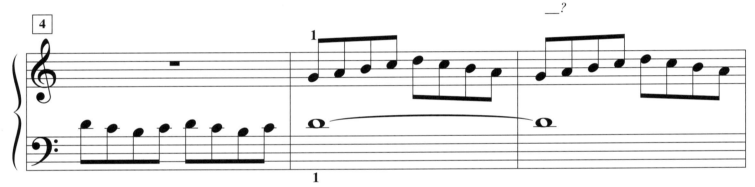

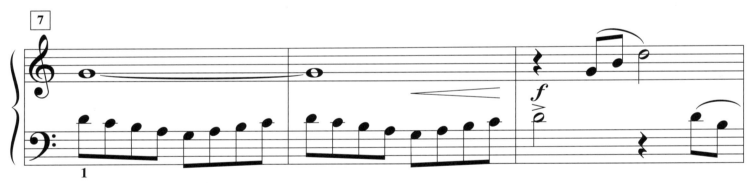

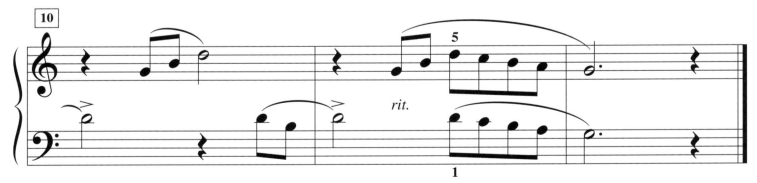

 DISCOVERY   Transpose *Finger Fanfare* to the notes of the **C pentascale**.

PLAY VIDEO

FF1302

■ Sightread these **G major pentascale** melodies.

■ Then, add harmony by writing **G** or **Gsus4** in the boxes. Listen and let your ears guide you.

■ Lastly, play each melody with the chords.

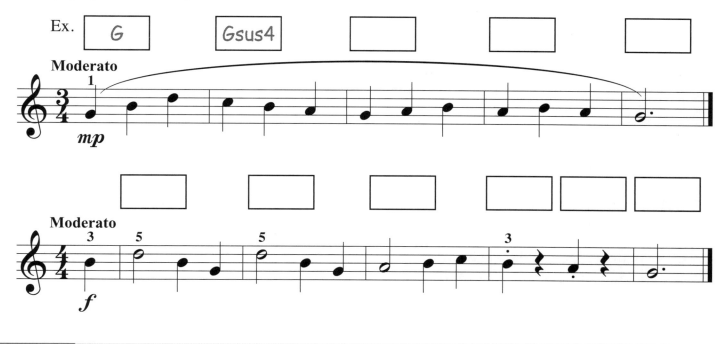

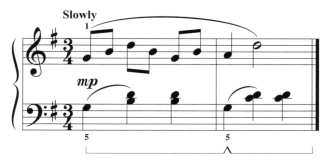

Your teacher (or friend) will play a short example that will end on the
G or **Gsus4** chord. Circle the correct answer for the last chord.
Hint: The **G** chord sounds *restful* and **complete**.
      The **Gsus4** chord sounds *restless* and **incomplete**.

a. G   **b.** G   **c.** G   **d.** G

    Gsus4   Gsus4   Gsus4   Gsus4

For Teacher Use Only (The examples may be played in any order.)

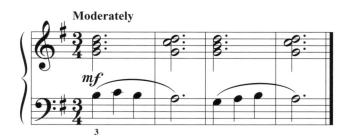

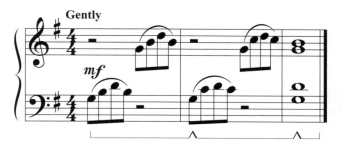

Sharps and Flats

Half Step

A **half step** is from one key to the very *closest* key.

■ Play these half steps on the piano.
Find and play several more half steps.

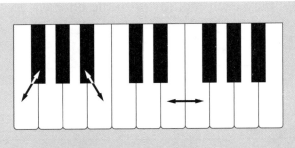

The Sharp ♯

A **sharp** means to play the key that is a **half step HIGHER**.

■ Play these keys up the keyboard while naming them aloud. Use R.H. finger 2.

Notice that E♯=F   Notice that B♯=C

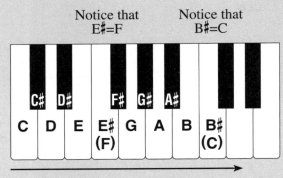

C# D# F# G# A#
C D E E♯ G A B B♯
(F) (C)

Warm-up with Sharps

■ Play slowly with the fingering given.

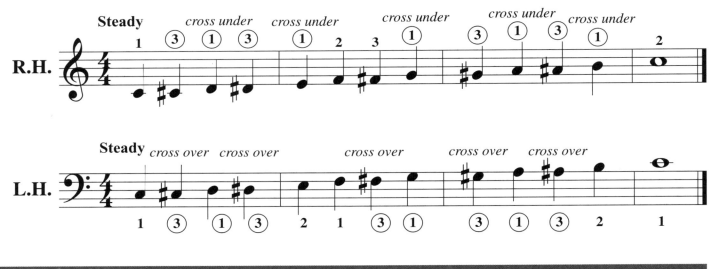

Rules for Sharps (See page 105)

■ A sharp carries through an entire measure, but not past a bar line. (*See measure 14*)
In a new measure, the sharp must be written again.

Note: Flats are introduced on page 108.

PLAY VIDEO

Half-Time Band

With pep

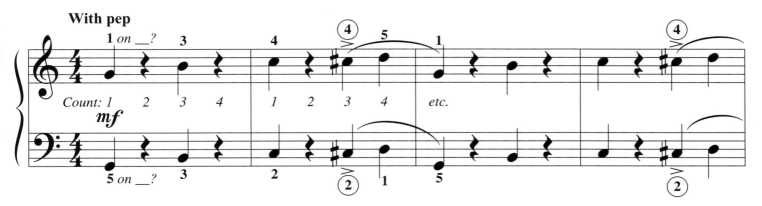

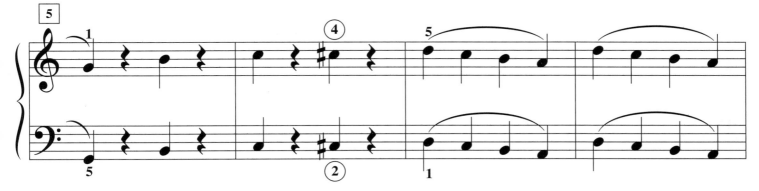

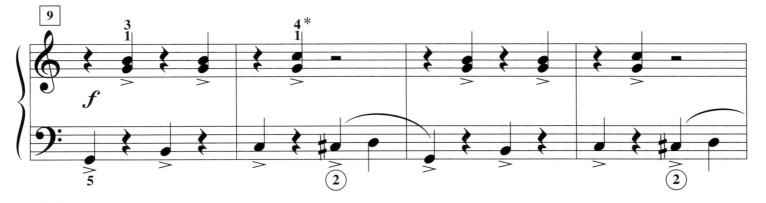

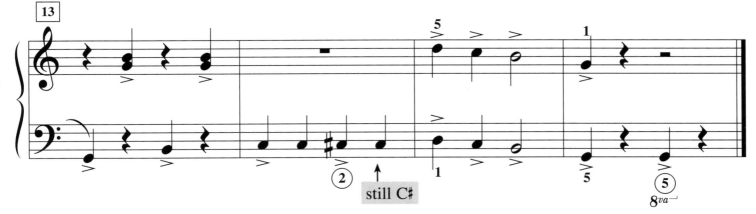

still C♯

 Name the pentascale used above: _____
Transpose *Half-Time Band* to the notes of the **C pentascale**.

PLAY VIDEO

*This is the interval of a 4th. 4ths are presented on page 116.

Greensleeves

English Folk Song
arranged

Gently moving

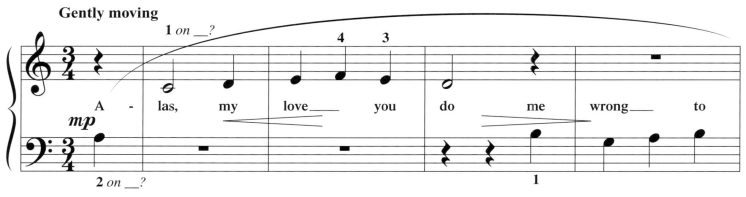

A - las, my love___ you do me wrong___ to

cast me off___ dis - cour - teous - ly. And I have

Teacher Duet: (Student plays *1 octave higher*)

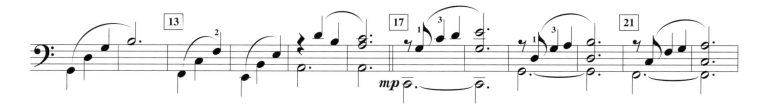

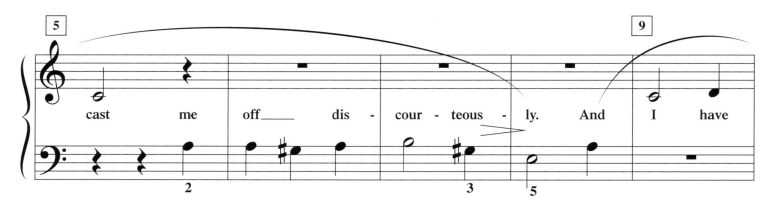

PLAY VIDEO

FF1302

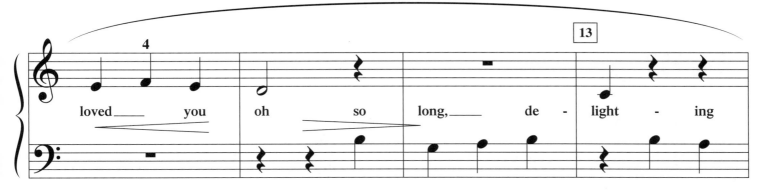

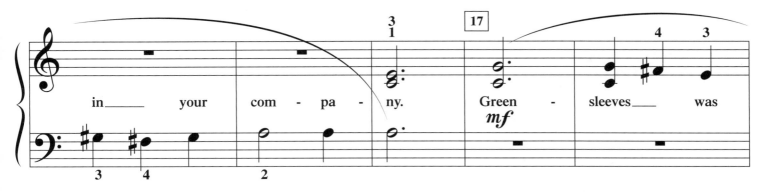

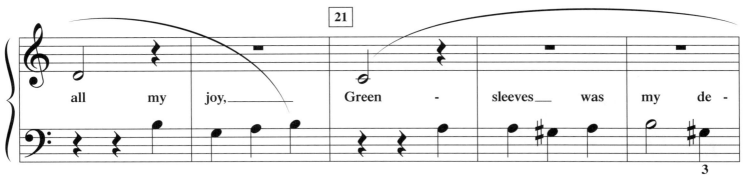

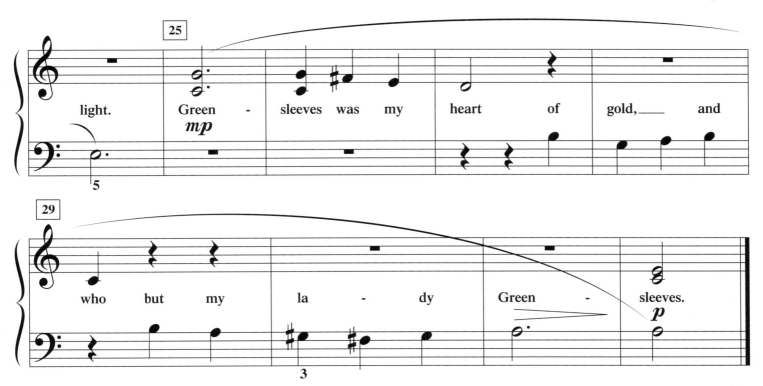

 DISCOVERY   How many beats does the **whole rest** receive in this song?

The Flat ♭

A **flat** means to play the key that is
a **half step LOWER**.

■ Play these keys down the keyboard while
naming them aloud. Use R.H. finger 2.

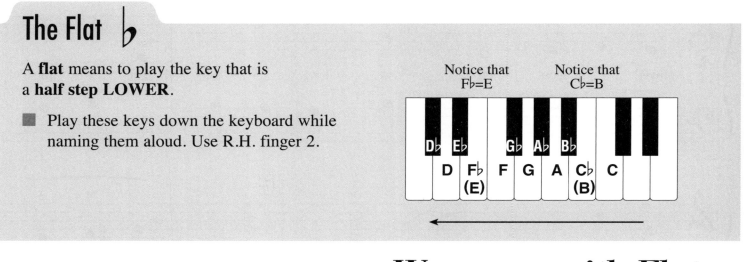

Notice that
F♭=E

Notice that
C♭=B

■ Play slowly with the fingering given.

Warm-up with Flats

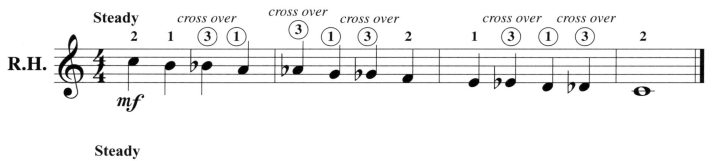

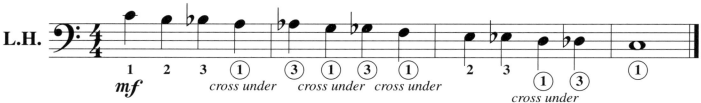

Teacher Duet for *Romance*, page 109: (Student plays *1 octave higher*)

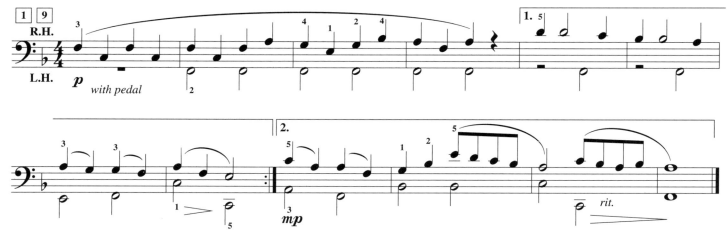

PLAY VIDEO

FF1302

Rules for Flats

- A flat carries through an entire measure, but not past a bar line. (*See measure 3*)

- In a new measure, the flat must be written again.

Romance
(from *A Little Night Music*)

Wolfgang Amadeus Mozart
(1756-1791, Austria)
arranged

DISCOVERY The 8th notes in this piece begin on: **beat 1   2   3   4** (*circle one*)

PLAY VIDEO

The Natural

A natural cancels a sharp or a flat.
A natural is always a white key.

Sometimes a natural is written as a reminder to play
a white key in a new measure. (*See measure 6*)

This is called a "courtesy" natural.

Sleeping Beauty Waltz

Peter Ilyich Tchaikovsky
(1840-1893, Russia)
arranged

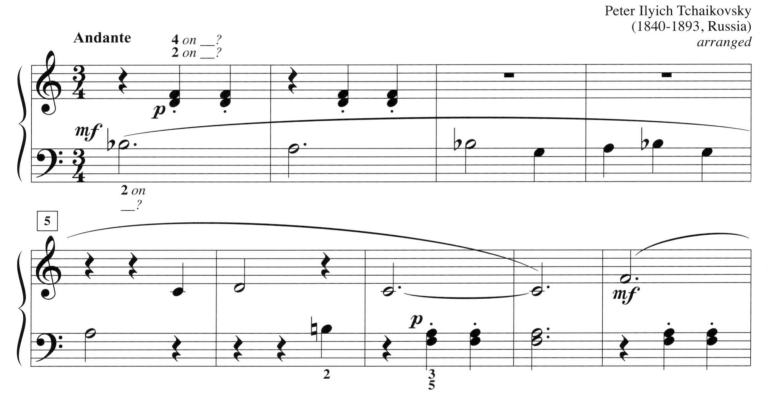

Teacher Duet: (Student plays *1 octave higher*, without pedal)

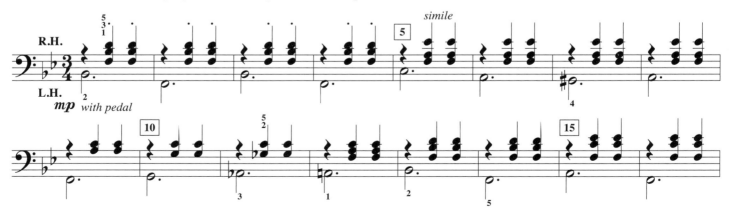

110   FF1302

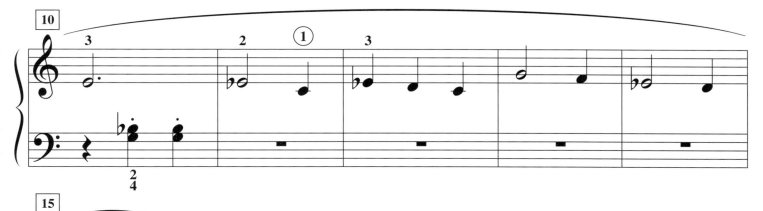

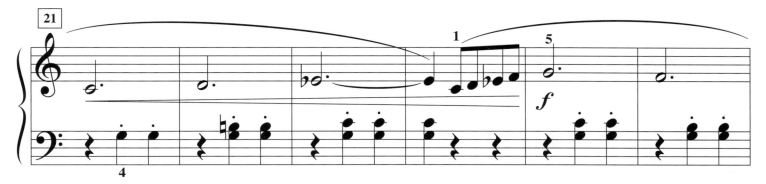

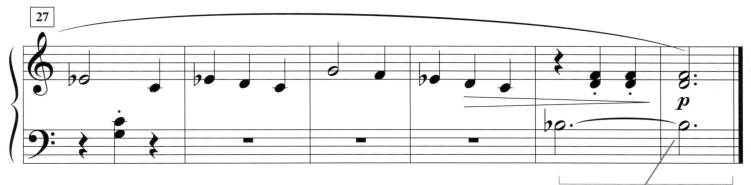

Because of the tie, the flat does not need to be written again in the last measure.

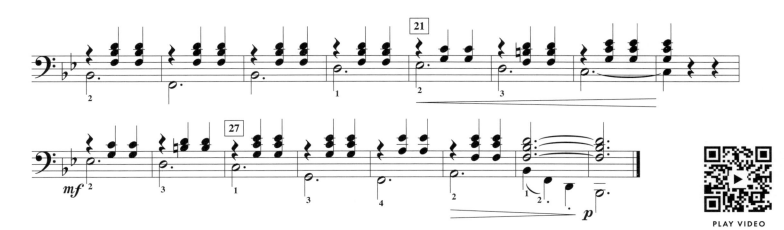

PLAY VIDEO

Whole Steps

A **whole step** is made of two half steps.
Think of a whole step as two keys with one key in between.

■ Find and play these whole steps on the piano.

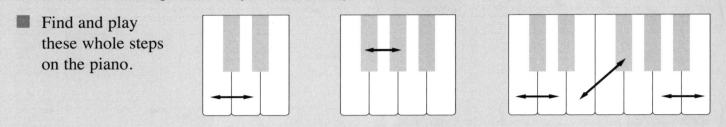

This piece depicts rumbling mountain thunder, rain, and then emerging sunshine.

■ The opening four measures are *whole steps*, starting with the **lowest C–D** on the keyboard.

■ Observe all the dynamic markings for a "colorful" sound.

3 2
└ L.H. ┘

Summer Mountain Rain

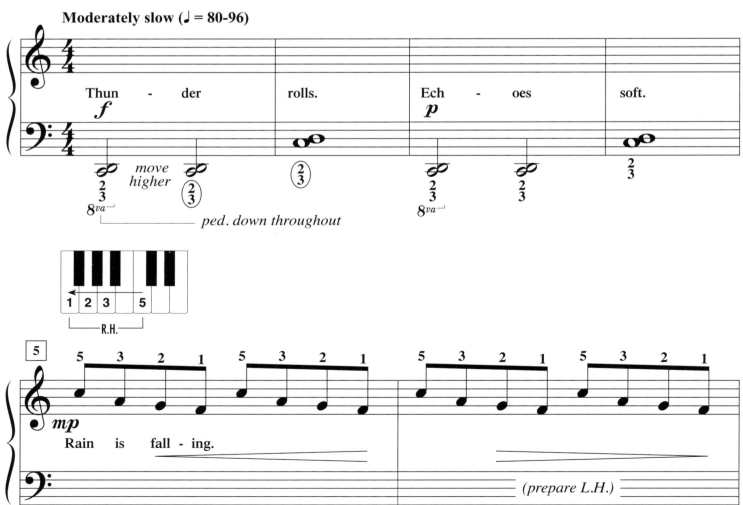

Moderately slow (♩ = 80-96)

Thun - der   rolls.   Ech - oes   soft.
f   *p*

move higher

ped. down throughout

Rain   is   fall - ing.
mp

(prepare L.H.)

FF1302

PLAY VIDEO

Two Kinds of 2nds

The notes of a scale move up or down by **2nds**.
A 2nd may be a *whole step* or *half step*.

Major pentascales (5-note scales) use this pattern:

Whole Step - Whole Step - Half Step - Whole Step

■ Study the keyboard diagram to the right.
Notice the **W W H W** pattern.

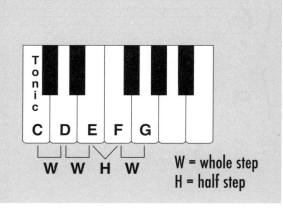

Major Pentascale Study

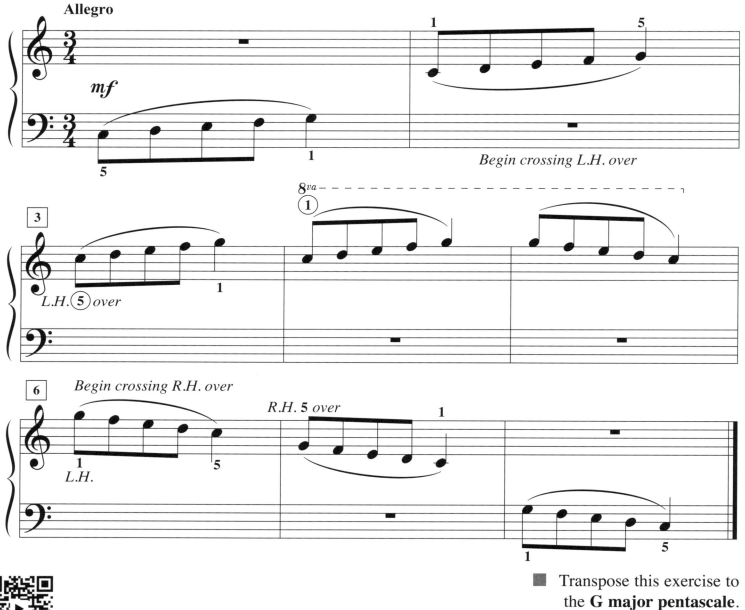

Allegro

mf

5

1   5

Begin crossing L.H. over

3

L.H. ⑤ *over*

1

8*va*
①

6   *Begin crossing R.H. over*

R.H. **5** *over*

1   5

L.H.

1

1   5

■ Transpose this exercise to
the **G major pentascale**.

PLAY VIDEO

FF1302

The **Whole-Whole-Half-Whole** pattern will help you learn the **D** and **A** major pentascales. Memorize the look and feel of these patterns.

■ Practice hands alone, then hands together.

D and A Major Pentascales

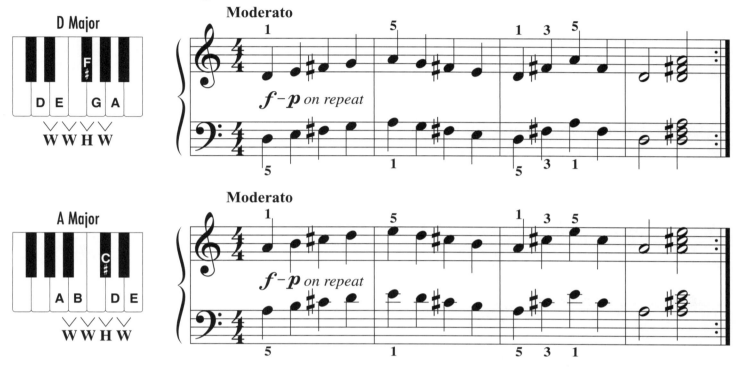

More Major Pentascales

■ Transpose the warm-up above to other major pentascales.

The keyboard diagrams in the *Major Pentascale Appendix* (pages 176-177) will guide you.
Note: There are 12 major pentascales. Gradually learn and memorize each.

C G D A E B F♯ (G♭) C♯ (D♭) A♭ E♭ B♭ F

Teacher Duet: (Student plays *1 octave higher*)

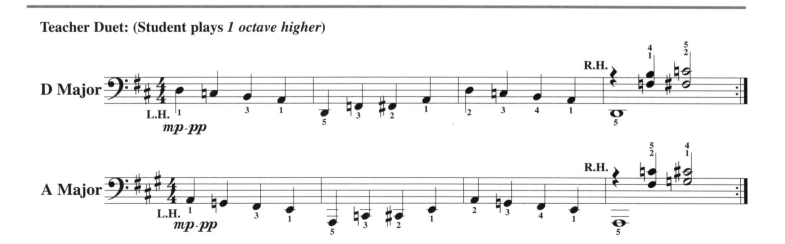

Intervals: 4ths, 5ths, 6ths

Intervals are easy to measure at the keyboard. Count the **number of white keys** (or letter names), including the *first* and *last* key. This is the number (size) of the interval.

The Interval of a 4th

A 4th spans 4 letter names.

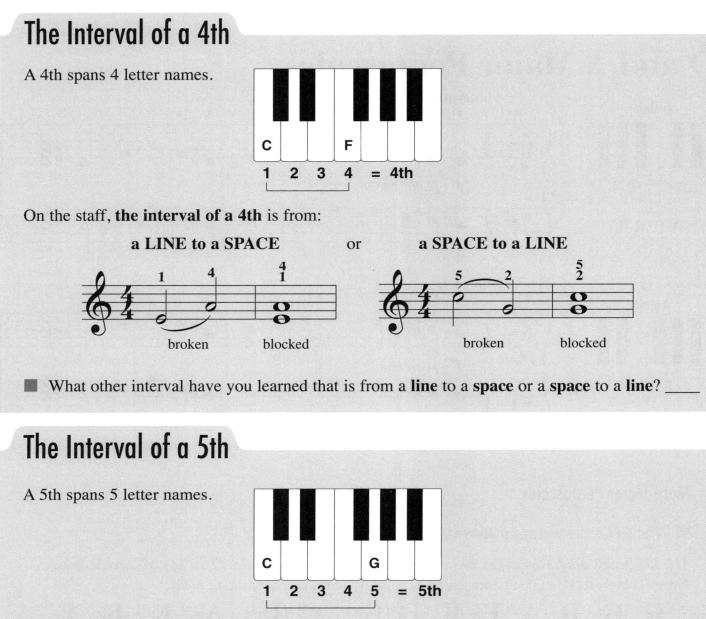

On the staff, **the interval of a 4th** is from:

a LINE to a SPACE   or   **a SPACE to a LINE**

broken   blocked   broken   blocked

■ What other interval have you learned that is from a **line** to a **space** or a **space** to a **line**? _____

The Interval of a 5th

A 5th spans 5 letter names.

On the staff, **the interval of a 5th** is from:

a LINE to a LINE   or   **a SPACE to a SPACE**

broken   blocked   broken   blocked

■ What other interval have you learned that is from a **line** to a **line** or a **space** to a **space**? _____

Note: 6ths are introduced on page 122.

PLAY VIDEO

FF1302

Focus on Fourths (4ths)

To draw an interval, count the starting note and each line and space.

■ Draw a **4th** *above* these line notes.

■ Then play each. Listen to the sound.

Think: **line** *skip-a-line* **to a space**

■ Draw a **4th** *below* these space notes.

■ Then play each. Listen to the sound.

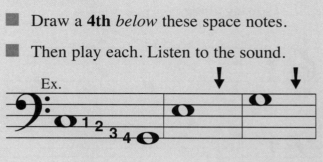

Think: **space** *skip-a-space* **to a line**

Promenade
(from *Pictures at an Exhibition*)

Modest Mussorgsky
(1839–1881, Russia)
arranged

DISCOVERY Circle all the **4ths**. (There are 8.)
(Remember to include the intervals between the staves.)

PLAY VIDEO

Teacher Duet: (Student plays *1 octave higher*)

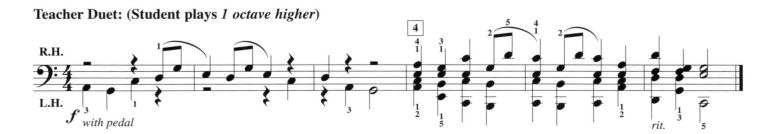

**Hold the damper pedal
down throughout the piece.**

Water Lilies

Flowing along

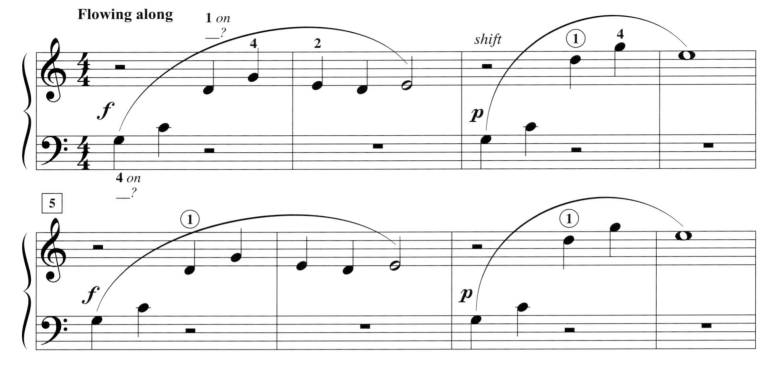

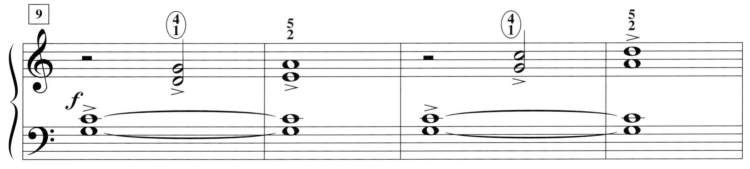

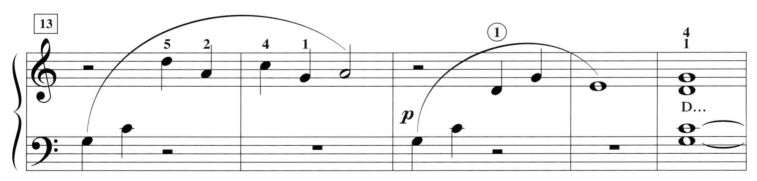

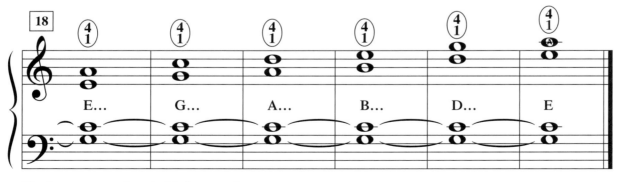

The lower note of each 4th is named.
This may guide your thumb.

PLAY VIDEO

FF1302

■ For the ending of this piece, the top note is *tied*
(R.H. finger 4) while fingers 1 and 2 move from **D** to **E**.

Danny Boy

Words by Fred E. Weatherly
Irish melody

DISCOVERY How many musical phrases are in this arrangement of *Danny Boy?*

PLAY VIDEO

Focus on Fifths (5ths)

■ Draw a **5th** *above* these line notes.

■ Then play each. Listen to the "open" sound.

■ Draw a **5th** *below* these space notes.

■ Then play each. Listen to the sound.

Think: **line** *skip-a-line* **to a line**

Think: **space** *skip-a-space* **to a space**

■ Before playing, name the intervals
(**2nd**, **3rd**, **4th**, or **5th**) in the blanks.

New Age Sounds

Andante

DISCOVERY

Name the pentascale used above: _____
Transpose *New Age Sounds* to the notes of the **D major pentascale**.

PLAY VIDEO

FF1302

An **aria** is a vocal piece — a song. Many arias are from operas — dramas in which music is an essential part. Operas feature arias, choruses, and orchestral playing.

Aria
(from *The Marriage of Figaro*)

Wolfgang Amadeus Mozart
(1756-1791, Austria)
arranged

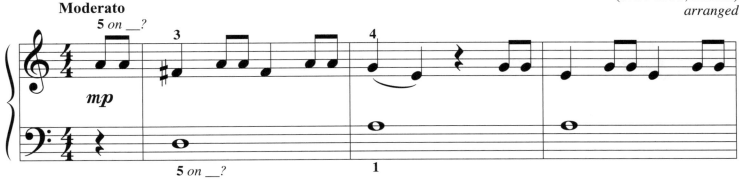

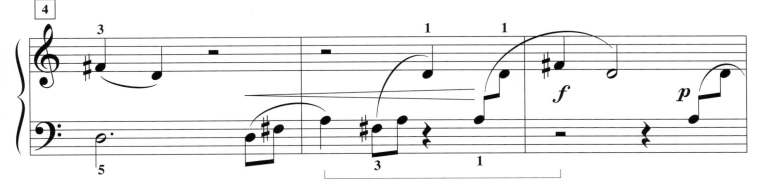

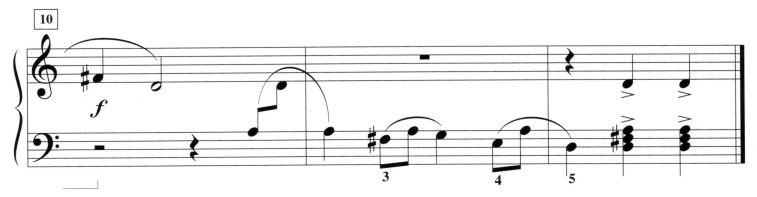

Name the pentascale used above: _____
Name the three letter names used in *measures 4, 5, and 6*.
What **major chord** do these notes form?

PLAY VIDEO

The Interval of a 6th

A **sixth (6th)** spans 6 keys and 6 letter names.

On the staff, the **interval of a 6th** is from:

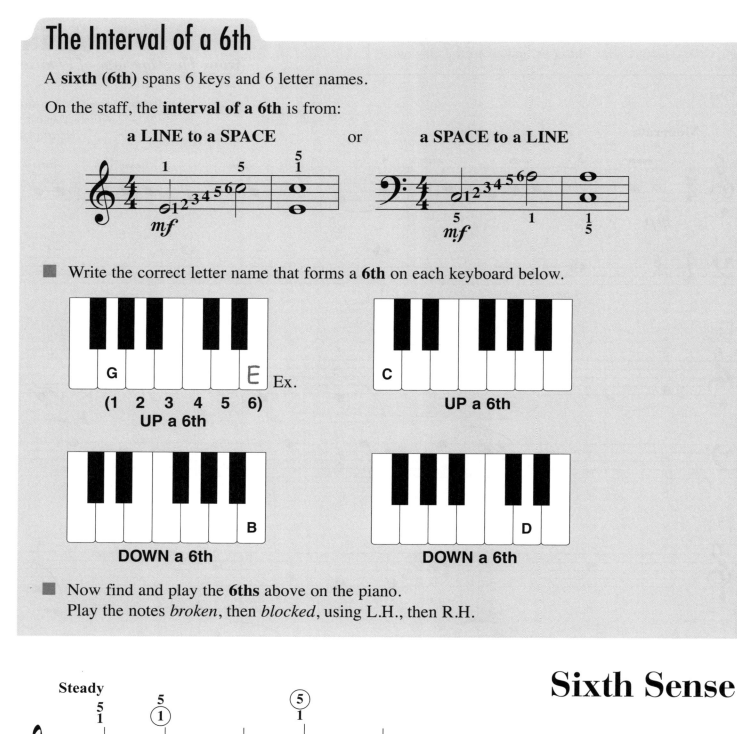

a LINE to a SPACE   or   a SPACE to a LINE

■ Write the correct letter name that forms a **6th** on each keyboard below.

G   E Ex.
(1 2 3 4 5 6)
UP a 6th

C
UP a 6th

B
DOWN a 6th

D
DOWN a 6th

■ Now find and play the **6ths** above on the piano.
  Play the notes *broken*, then *blocked*, using L.H., then R.H.

Sixth Sense

Steady

mf

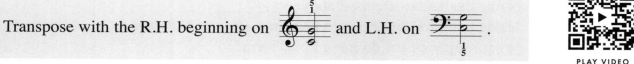

DISCOVERY   Transpose with the R.H. beginning on and L.H. on .

PLAY VIDEO

FF1302

The Lion Sleeps Tonight

■ Name the pentascale used below: _____

Words and Music by George David Weiss,
Hugo Peretti, Luigi Creatore, and Solomon Linda

Teacher Duet: (Student plays *1 octave higher,* without pedal)

PLAY VIDEO

Nobody Knows the Trouble I've Seen

Spiritual

Find two places where the hands play in **parallel motion**. (See p. 68)

PLAY VIDEO

FF1302

■ Play the thumb *lightly*. This will help
bring out the accented notes.

L.H. Interval Study

R.H. Interval Study

Hands-Together Interval Study

■ Play the R.H. *legato*—with no break in the sound.

■ Lift the L.H. slightly on each quarter rest to prepare the next interval.

 **DISCOVERY** Transpose each exercise on this page to the **D** and **A major pentascales**.
For additional pentascales, see page 176.

PLAY VIDEO

 FF1302

1. Write a whole note a **4th up** or **down** from each note. (See p. 116.) Then name both notes.

down a 4th   up a 4th   down a 4th   up a 4th   up a 4th

_____ _____   _____ _____   _____ _____   _____ _____   _____ _____

2. Write a whole note a **5th up** or **down** from each note. (See p. 116.) Then name both notes.

up a 5th   down a 5th   down a 5th   up a 5th   down a 5th

_____ _____   _____ _____   _____ _____   _____ _____   _____ _____

3. Identify each interval as a **5th** or **6th**. Then play each on the piano. Play _mf_.

____   ____   ____   ____   ____

4. Sightread the two melodies below at a slow tempo. Watch for **4ths**, **5ths**, and **6ths**.

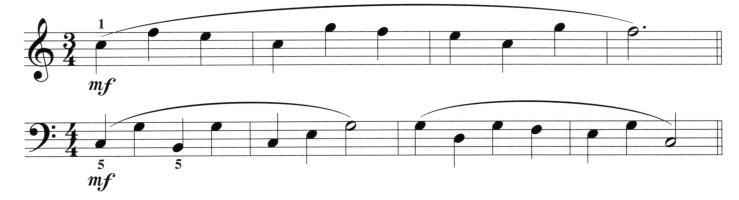

EAR TRAINING

Your teacher (or a friend) will play example **a** or **b**.
Circle the musical example you hear.

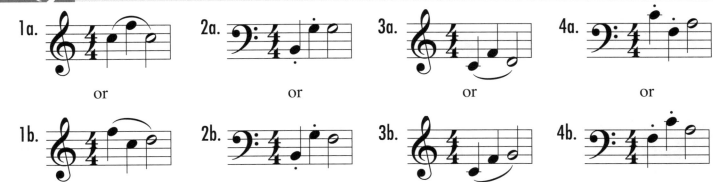

The C Major Scale

The C major scale is the C pentascale plus two added notes: A and B (and the higher C, tonic). All seven letters of the music alphabet are used in a major scale.

A major scale is composed of **whole steps** *except* for two **half steps** between scale degrees 3–4 and 7–8.

C major pentascale — two new notes

scale degrees: 1   2   3   half step   4   5   6   7   *leads to*   8 (1)

tonic   dominant   leading tone   tonic

C Scale Warm-ups

Slow, steady

R.H.

thumb under   *shift hand to new position*   cross over

Slow, steady   *thumb under*   *shift hand to new position*   *cross over*

L.H.

Key of C Roadmap

Steady

Ton - ic up to dom - i - nant.   Ton - ic up to dom - i - nant.

Ton - ic up to dom - i - nant and lead - ing tone to C!

DISCOVERY Using only R.H. finger 3, play the C major scale and stop on the *leading tone*. Do you hear how the *leading tone* pulls up to the *tonic* note C? Complete the scale by playing *the tonic*.

PLAY VIDEO

FF1302

One Octave C Major Scale

■ Practice s-l-o-w-l-y and *listen* for an even tone!

■ Memorize the fingering for the C major scale.

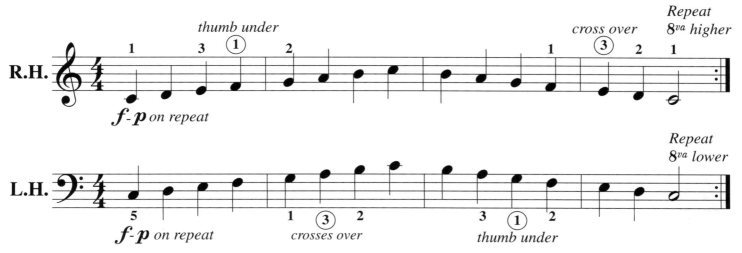

Metronome Practice

Put a ✓ in the blank when you can play the C major scale **hands alone** at these tempi.
Play *ascending* (going up), then *descending* (going down) as in the above examples.

legato ♩ = 88 ____	*legato* ♩ = 112 ____	*legato* ♩ = 144 ____
staccato ♩ = 88 ____	*staccato* ♩ = 112 ____	*staccato* ♩ = 144 ____

Review of Parallel and Contrary Motion

parallel motion — notes moving in the *same* direction. (See p. 68)

contrary motion — notes moving in *opposite* directions. (See below.)
Notice the **same** fingers play together in both hands.

C Major Scale in Contrary Motion

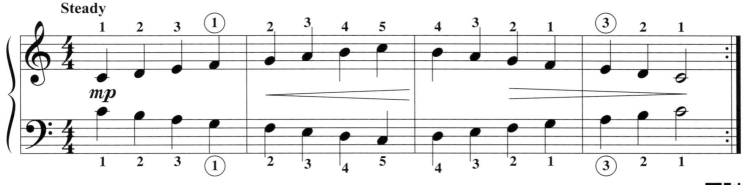

Playing in the Key of C Major

A piece in the **Key of C major** uses the notes of the
C major scale (or pentascale) for its melody and harmony.

A piece in the Key of C will almost always end on C in
the bass clef.

Vive la France!

French Folk Song

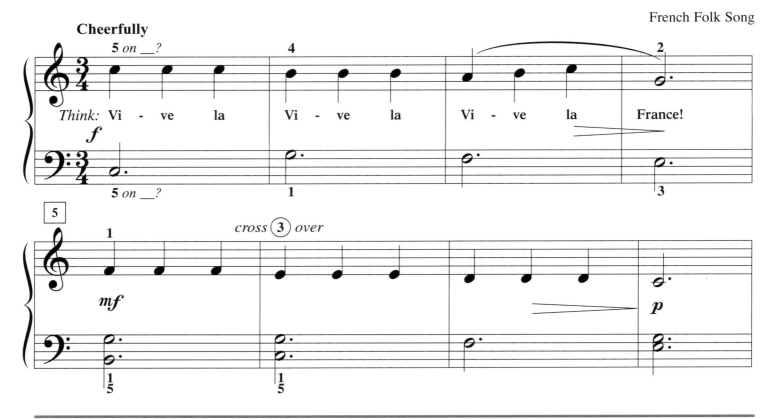

Teacher Duet: (Student plays *2 octaves higher*)

FF1302

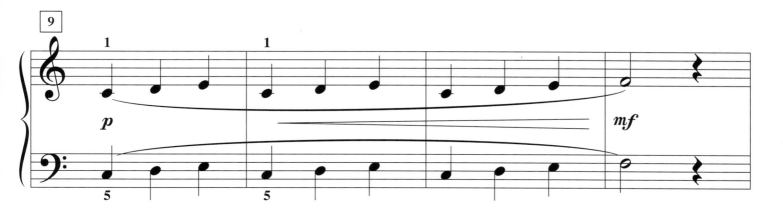

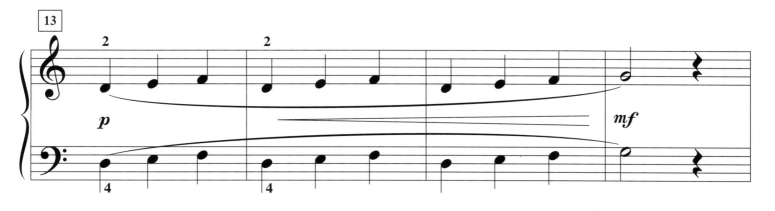

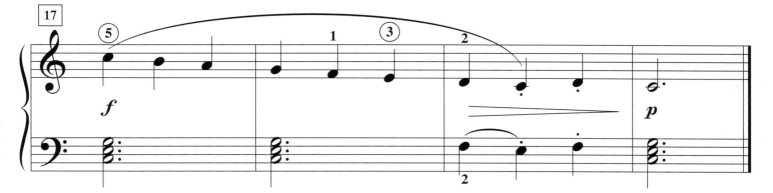

 DISCOVERY Point out two lines of music where the hands play in **parallel motion**.

PLAY VIDEO

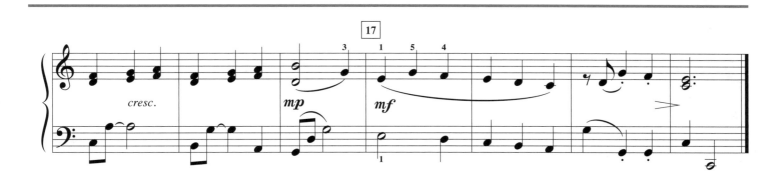

3-Minute Technique

Review of Melody and Harmony (See page 54)

In this piece the R.H. plays a *melody* which uses the C major scale.

The L.H. plays the *harmony* (notes or chords which support the melody).
The harmony should be played *softer* than the melody.

■ Play the L.H. intervals lightly, on the surface of the key.
Notice the **dynamic markings** for each hand.

Scale Waltz
Key of C Major

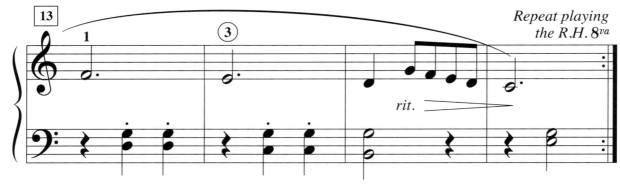

Repeat playing
the R.H. 8va

rit.

PLAY VIDEO

FF1302

1. Write the **R.H. fingering** for the C major scale.
Write **T** (tonic), **D** (dominant), or **LT** (leading tone) below the correct notes.
Mark the *half steps* between scale degrees 3–4 and 7–8 with a wedge (∨) below the notes.

fingering:

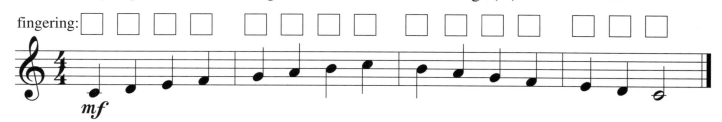

2. Do the above three steps for the **L.H.** C major scale.

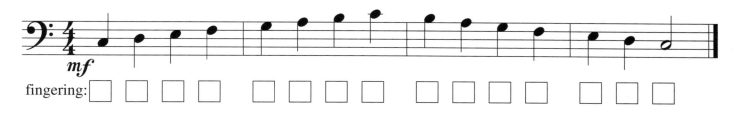

fingering:

Improvisation with Sixths (6ths)

▪ Your teacher (or a friend) will play the duet below. First, *listen* and feel the beat.

▪ When you are ready, use only white keys and improvise a short piece using **blocked 6ths** in the mid-range of the piano. Use mostly **o** notes. Begin and end with this **6th**: C E

Teacher Duet:

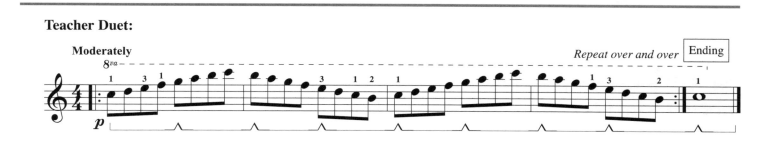

 EAR TRAINING Close your eyes and listen. Your teacher (or a friend) will play a short example that will end on the *tonic* or *dominant*. Circle the correct answer.
Note: Each example begins on the *tonic*.

a. tonic

dominant

b. tonic

dominant

c. tonic

dominant

d. tonic

dominant

For Teacher Use Only (The examples may be played in any order.)

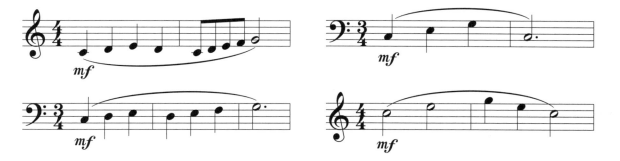

The G7 Chord

G7 Chord in Root Position

The G7 chord is a four-note chord built up in **3rds** from **G**.
When G (the root) is the *lowest* note, the chord is in ROOT POSITION.

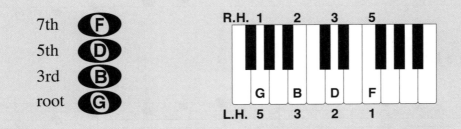

7th F
5th D
3rd B
root G

R.H. 1   2   3   5
G   B   D   F
L.H. 5   3   2   1

Inverted G7 Chord

Then notes of the **G7** chord are often *inverted* (rearranged) to form a **3-note G7 chord**.

7th F   F G
5th D   The 5th is omitted.
3rd B   B
root G   G moves up an octave.

R.H.   1   4 5
B   F G
L.H.   5   2 1

G7 = V7 in the Key of C

Because G is *scale degree 5* (the dominant - V) in the Key of C, the **G7 chord** is called the
V7 ("five-seven") or **Dominant 7** chord in the Key of C.

Inverted G7 (V7) for L.H.

- Play a 5th in the C major scale.

- Move finger 5 a **half step lower** (B).
  (This expands the interval to a 6th.)

- Add **L.H. finger 2** (scale degree 4).

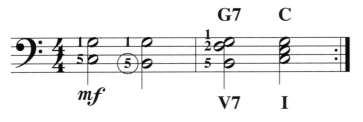

G7   C

mf

V7   I

Inverted G7 (V7) for R.H.

- Play a 5th in the C major scale.

- Move finger 1 a **half step lower** (B).
  (This expands the interval to a 6th.)

- Add **R.H. finger 4** (scale degree 4).

G7   C

mf

V7   I

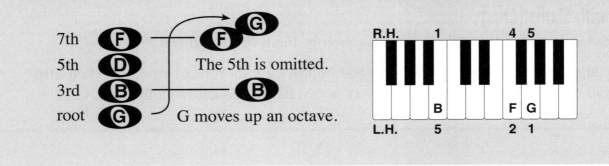

DISCOVERY Play a R.H. **C major pentascale** slowly up and down.
Harmonize each note with a L.H. **C** or **G7** chord.
Listen and let your ears guide you.

PLAY VIDEO

FF1302

Trumpet Voluntary
Key of C Major

■ Chord letter names (C, G7, etc.)
are *above* the staff. Roman numerals
(I, V7, etc.) are *below*.

Jeremiah Clarke
(1673-1707, England)
arranged

Dignified march

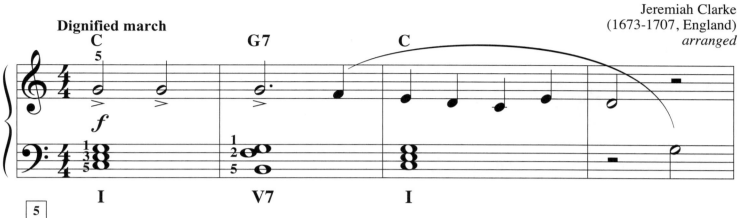

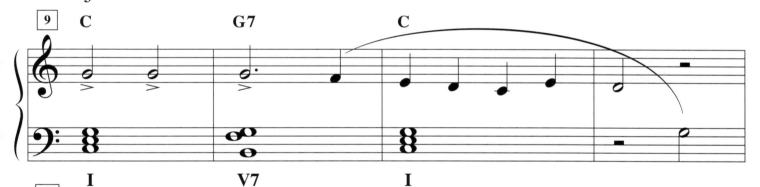

Teacher Duet: (Student plays *1 octave higher*)

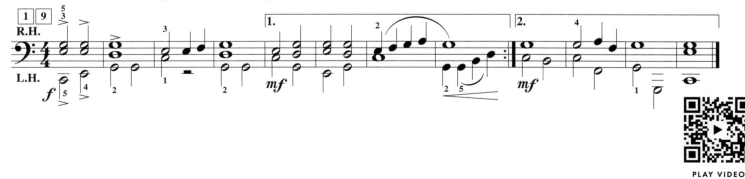

Finger Substitutions

Finger substitution means changing to a new finger on a *repeated note*.
This places the hand in a new location on the keys.

Warm-up

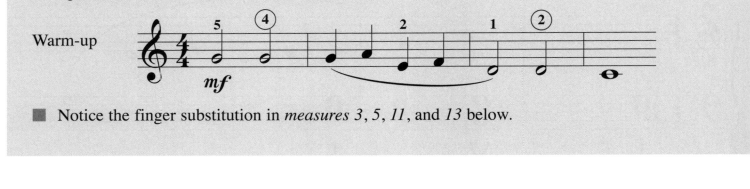

■ Notice the finger substitution in *measures 3*, *5*, *11*, and *13* below.

can-can — a lively French dance that features high
kicks performed by women in a chorus line.

Can-Can
Key of C Major

Jacques Offenbach
(1819-1880, France)
arranged

Allegro moderato (moderately fast)

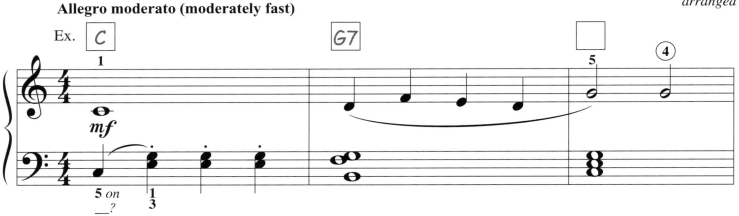

Teacher Duet: (Student plays *1 octave higher*)

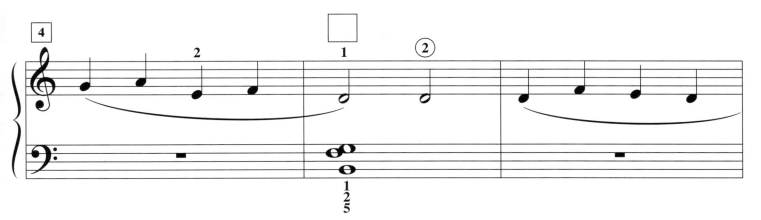

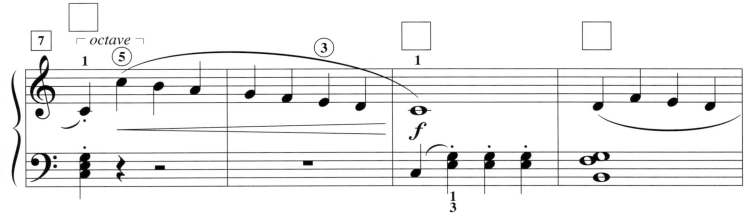

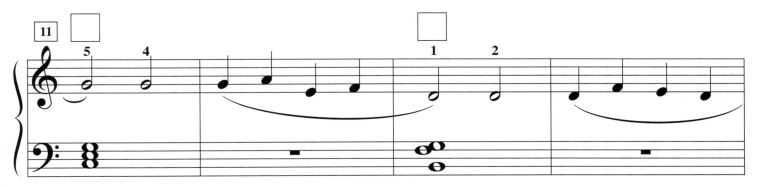

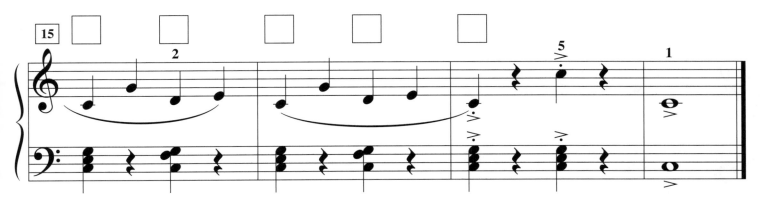

PLAY VIDEO

DISCOVERY Write chord symbols: **C**, **Csus4**, or **G7** in the boxes *above* the measures.

Waltz Chord Pattern

Play each example four times as a daily warm-up.

I Chord   **V7 Chord**   **V7 Chord**

Ice Skaters*

Emile Waldteufel
(1837-1915, France)
arranged

Gliding along

*original French title Les Patineurs

FF1302

On repeat, play R.H. 8va higher

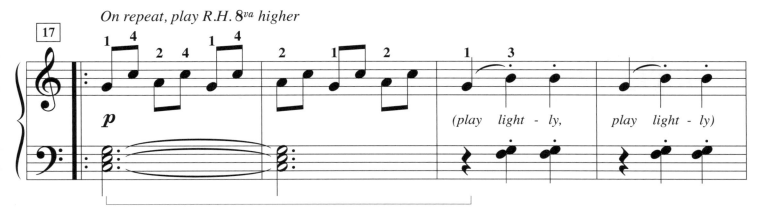

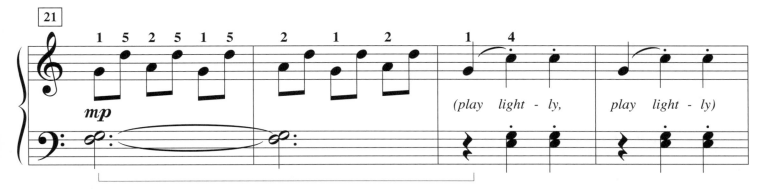

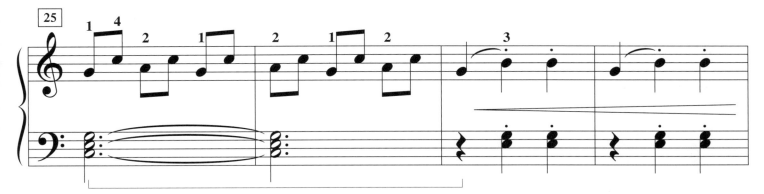

Chord Warm-ups

Blocked Chords

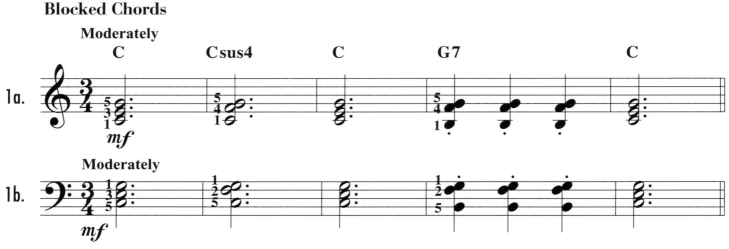

1a.

1b.

Can you play exercise **1a** and **1b** hands together?

Blocked and Broken Chords

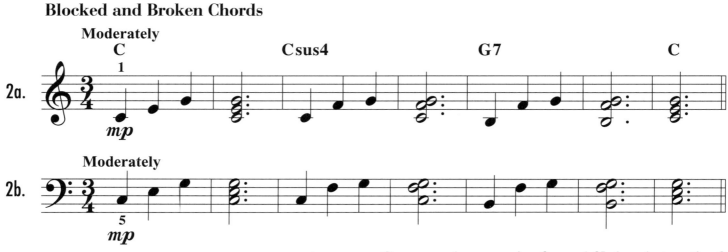

2a.

2b.

Can you play exercise **2a** and **2b** hands together?

Broken Chords

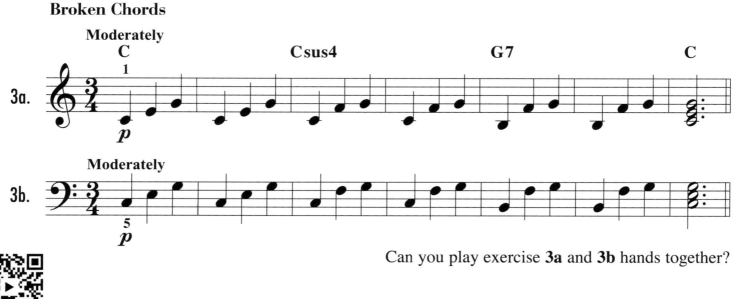

3a.

3b.

Can you play exercise **3a** and **3b** hands together?

PLAY VIDEO

FF1302

1. Write **C**, **Csus4**, or **G7** above each *blocked* or *broken* chord.

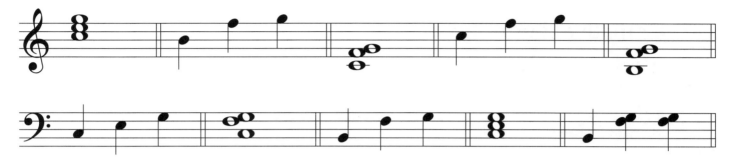

2. Write **1 + 2 + 3 + 4 +** below each measure. Then sightread, counting aloud.

Rather slowly

3. Play hands together slowly, reading the **chord letter names** (without written music).

   ▪ First play with *blocked* chords. (Hint: Count 3 beats for each measure.)
   ▪ Repeat using *broken* chords.

$\frac{3}{4}$ C | G7 | C | Csus4 | G7 | G7 | C :‖

 EAR TRAINING Your teacher will play a short example that will end with a **I** or **V7** chord.
Circle the chord that you hear at the end.
Hint: The **I chord** sounds finished or complete. The **V7 chord** sounds "restless."

a. I chord   **b.** I chord   **c.** I chord   **d.** I chord

   V7 chord   V7 chord   V7 chord   V7 chord

For Teacher Use Only (The examples may be played in any order.)

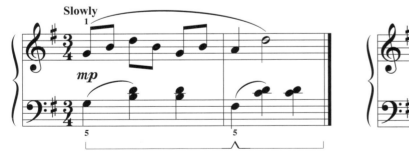

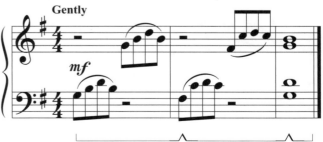

Primary Chords in C Major

The Primary Chords: I-IV-V

The **I**, **IV**, and **V** chords are called the *primary* chords.
They are built on scale degrees 1, 4, and 5 of the major scale.

chord letter names:	C			F	G			
scale degrees:	1	2	3	4	5	6	7	8 (1)
Roman numerals:	I			IV	V			
chord names:	tonic			subdominant	dominant			

The C, F, and G chords shown above are in **root position**.
Remember, this means the letter name of the chord is the bottom note.

Primary Chord Study

■ Practice and memorize, using the root position **C**, **F**, and **G chords**.

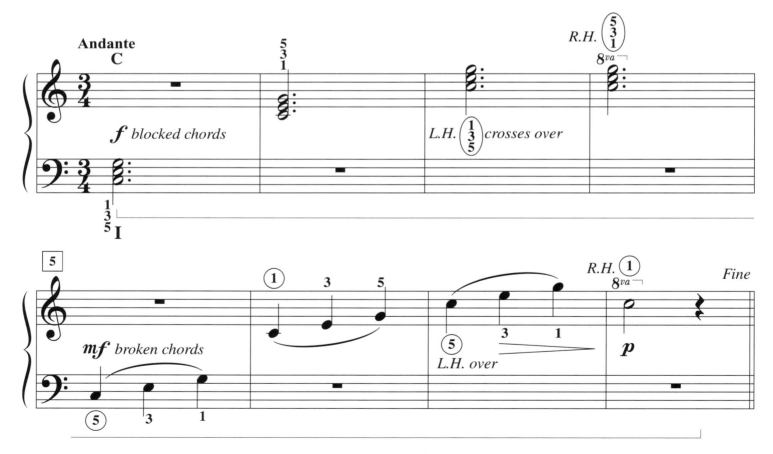

FF1302

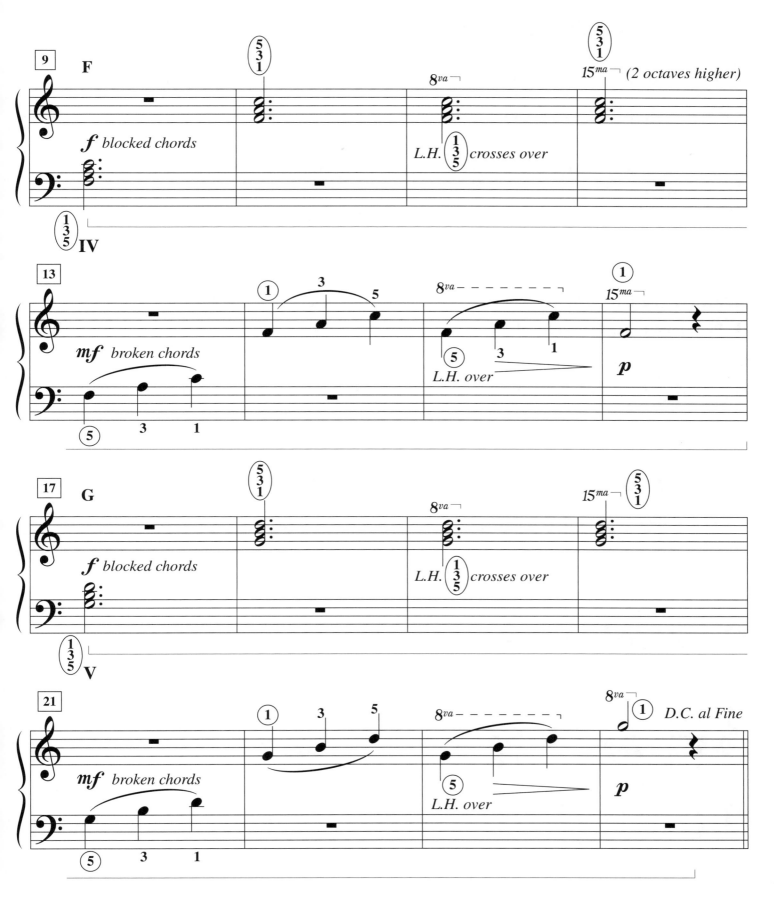

Inverting the IV Chord

To eliminate the leap from the **I** chord to the **IV chord**,
the notes of the IV chord can be rearranged, or inverted.

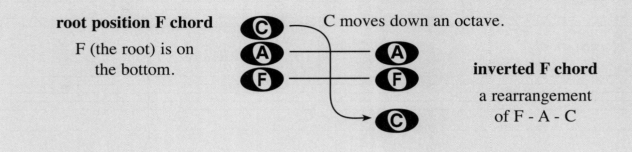

root position F chord

F (the root) is on
the bottom.

C moves down an octave.

inverted F chord

a rearrangement
of F - A - C

Inverted IV Chord for L.H.

■ Play a 5th in the C major scale.

■ The thumb moves UP a *whole step* (A).

■ L.H. finger 2 plays F (scale degree 4).

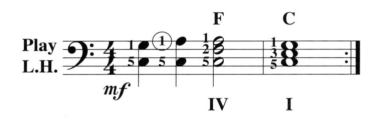

Inverted IV Chord for R.H.

■ Play a 5th in the C major scale.

■ Finger 5 moves UP a *whole step* (A).

■ R.H. finger 3 moves up a *half step* to F
(scale degree 4).

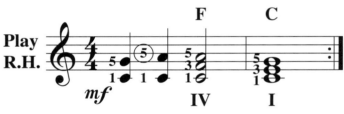

Notice the R.H. fingering!

IV Chord Warm-up in C

Steady

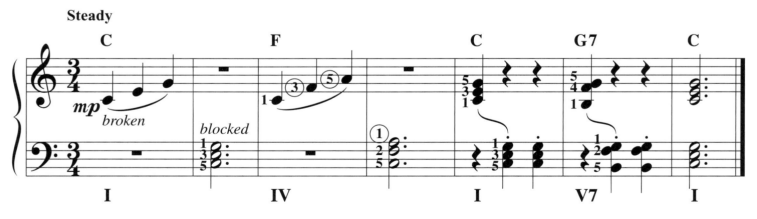

DISCOVERY Play a **C major pentascale** up and down s-l-o-w-l-y with your R.H.
Harmonize *each* note by playing a **C**, **F**, or **G7** chord with your L.H.
Use *inversions* for the F and G7 chords.

PLAY VIDEO

FF1302

■ Tap the rhythm for the R.H. on the closed keyboard cover.
  Count aloud, **"1-2-3-4."**

■ Play the R.H. melody alone, without chords.

■ Play hands together, slowly.

Rise and Shine
Key of C Major

Traditional

DISCOVERY Write **I**, **IV**, or **V7** below each chord.

Technique Hint

■ Play beats 2 and 3 lightly with the L.H., from the surface of the key.

Theme from
Trumpet Concerto
Key of C Major

Franz Joseph Haydn
(1732-1809, Austria)
arranged

Ex. C

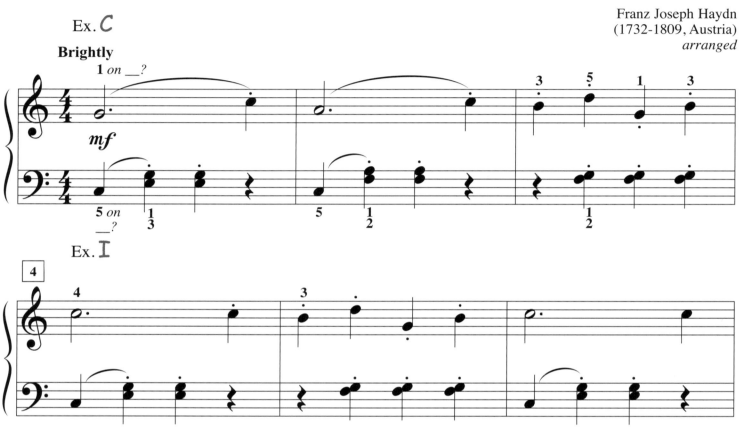

Ex. I

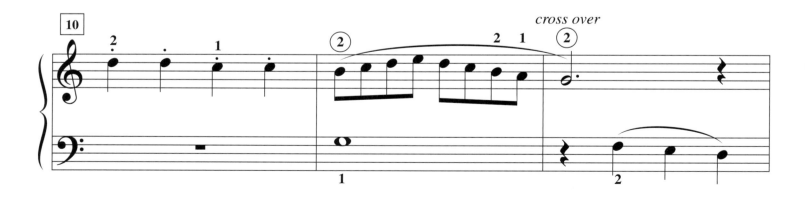

FF1302

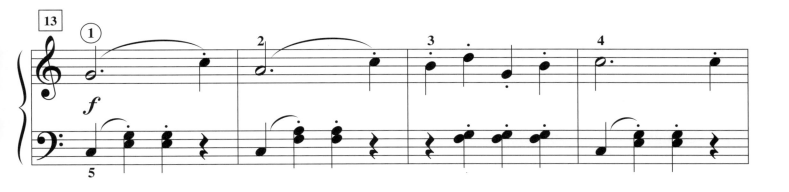

 For each chord, write **C**, **F**, or **G7** *above* the treble staff.
Then, write **I**, **IV**, or **V7** *below* each chord.

PLAY VIDEO

Accidentals ♯ ♭ ♮

Remember, the Key of C Major has no sharps or flats.

Sharps, flats, and naturals that are added to a piece are called **accidentals**.
Accidentals give "spice and color" by adding notes that are not in the major scale of the piece.

For example, the **D♯ upbeat** in *The Entertainer* is an accidental.

■ Learn the R.H. melody thoroughly before playing hands together.

■ Write **I**, **IV**, or **V7** in each box for *measures 1–7*. The treble staff notes will help you determine the chord. Some chords may be incomplete or broken. (See *measure 4*.)

The Entertainer
Key of C Major

Scott Joplin
(1869-1917, USA)
arranged

FF1302

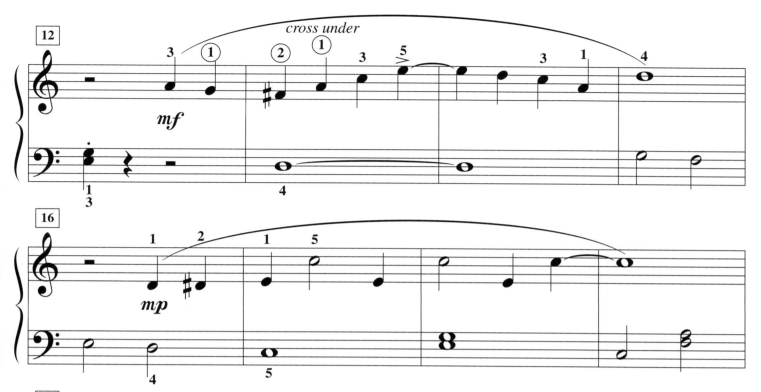

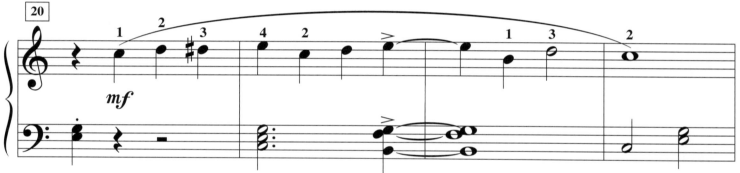

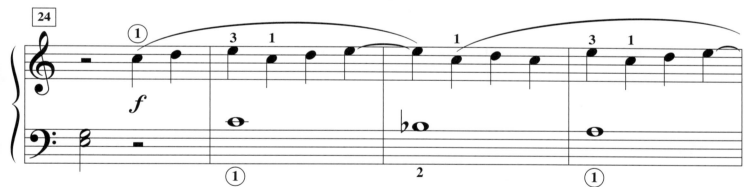

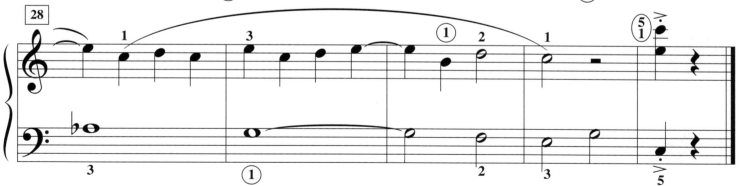

 **DISCOVERY**

Remember, a *phrase* is a musical sentence. (See p. 72)
Find 3 phrases with the interval of a **6th** in the melody.

PLAY VIDEO

Lead Sheet

In popular music, the "lead" means the melody.
A *lead sheet* consists of a melody *only*, with
chord symbols written above the staff.

Explore playing *melody* and *harmony* from a lead
sheet by following the directions below.

Chord References in C Major

Practice the chords used in *Home on the Range*.

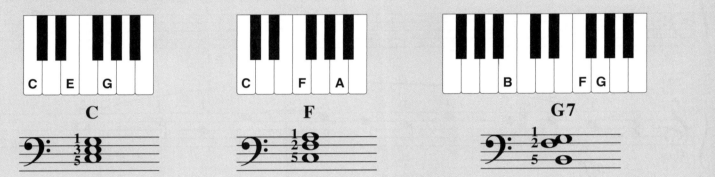

- Play the melody only with the damper pedal, as shown.
  (Pedal marks are usually not included as part of a lead sheet.)

- Then add L.H. **blocked chords** on *beat 1* of each measure as indicated by the chord symbols.
  (If no chord symbol is present, repeat the chord of the previous measure.)

Home on the Range

Traditional

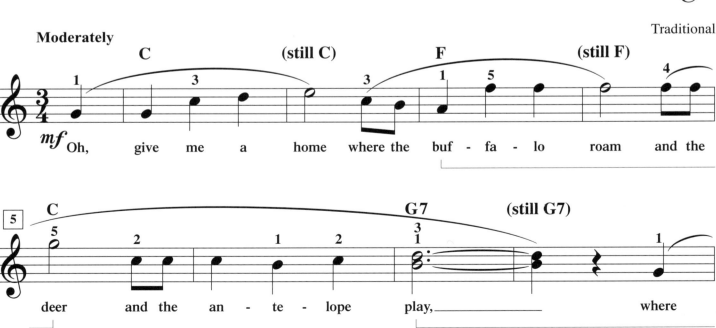

FF1302

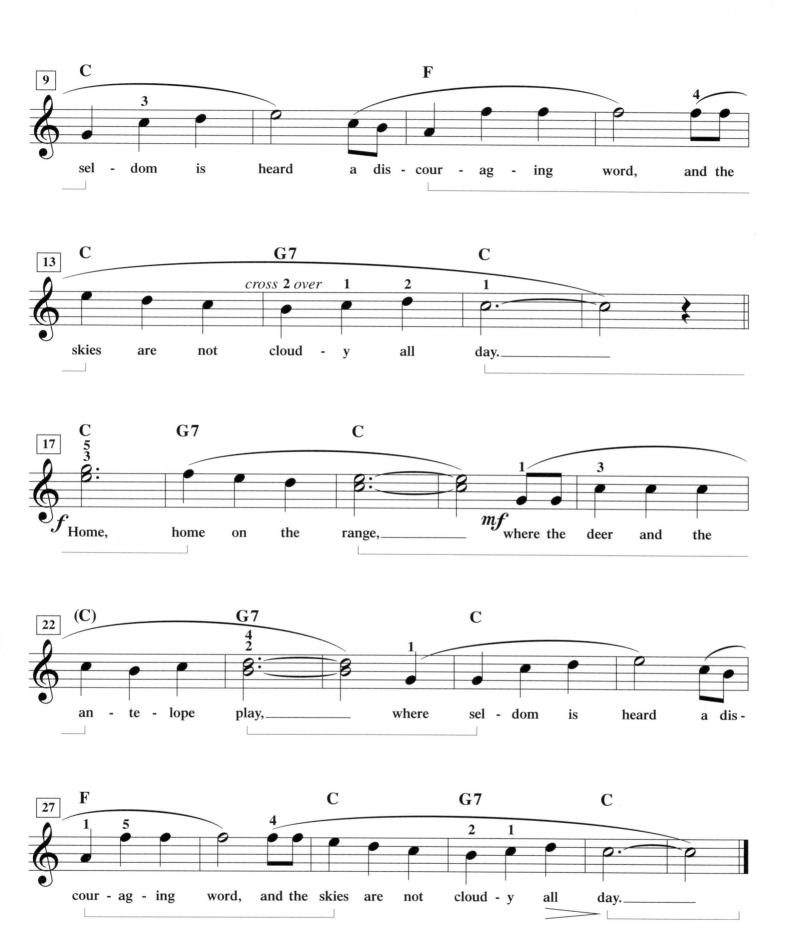

Technique Hint

■ Let your R.H. wrist gently lift, gracefully leading your hand to the next higher chord. The quarter rest will give you time to *prepare* the next chord.

Chord Etude
Key of C

Slow and peacefully

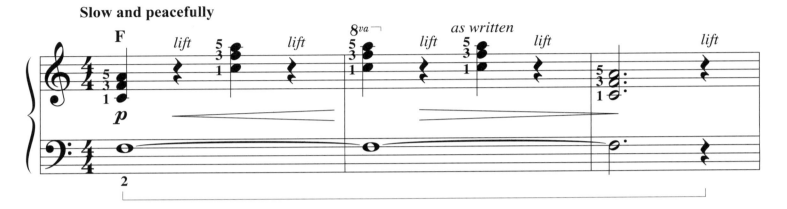

PLAY VIDEO

FF1302

Primary Chords in the Key of C Major

■ Draw a line connecting the chord letter names and Roman numerals shown on the left to the matching chords on the right.

■ Then write the **chord letter names** in the boxes given.

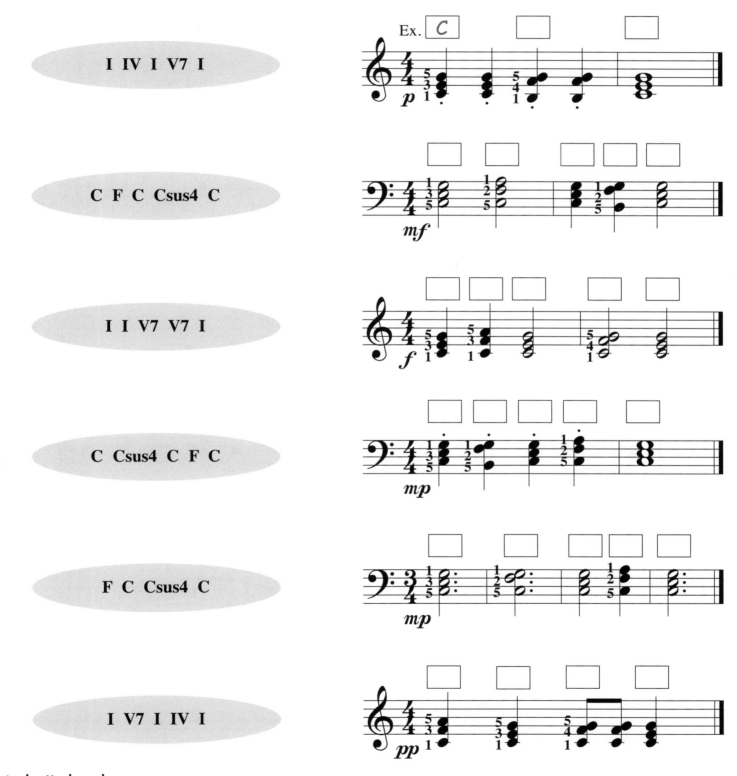

I IV I V7 I

C F C Csus4 C

I I V7 V7 I

C Csus4 C F C

F C Csus4 C

I V7 I IV I

At the Keyboard

■ With your L.H., play all the chords in the boxes on the left. You are reading **chord symbols**.

■ Then *sightread* the chords on the right with the correct hand. (Check the clef sign.)

The G Major Scale

The G Major Scale

The G major scale is the G pentascale plus two added notes: E and F-sharp (and the higher G, tonic).

Remember, a major scale is made up of all **whole steps** *except* for **half steps** between scale degrees 3–4, and 7–8.

G Scale Warm-ups

Key of G Roadmap

DISCOVERY Using only R.H. finger 3, play the G major scale and stop on the *leading tone*.
Do you hear how the *leading tone* pulls up to the *tonic* note G?
Complete the scale by playing the *tonic*.

PLAY VIDEO

FF1302

One Octave G Major Scale

■ Practice s-l-o-w-l-y and *listen* for an even tone!

■ **Memorize the fingering for the G major scale.**

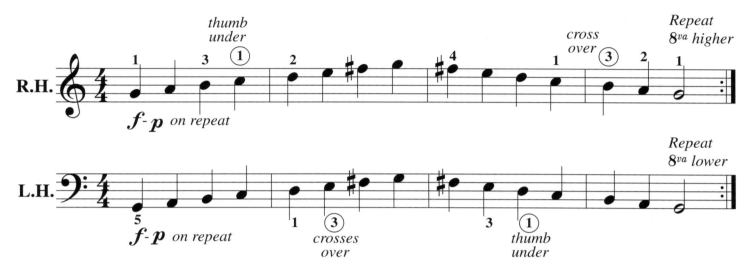

Metronome Practice

Put a ✓ in the blank when you can play the G major scale **hands alone** at these tempi.
Play each hand *ascending*, then *descending*.

legato	♩ = 88 ___	*legato*	♩ = 112 ___	*legato*	♩ = 144 ___
staccato	♩ = 88 ___	*staccato*	♩ = 112 ___	*staccato*	♩ = 144 ___

G Major Scale in Contrary Motion

■ Notice the **same** fingers play together in both hands for contrary motion.

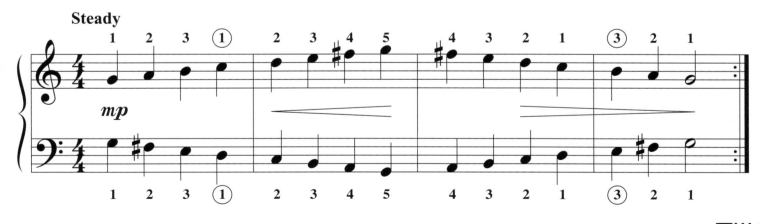

PLAY VIDEO

Key Signature for G Major

Since the G major scale has an *F-sharp*, a piece in the **Key of G major** will use F-sharps throughout. Remember, F-sharp is the *leading tone* in the Key of G major.

Instead of a sharp appearing before every F, a sharp is written **on the F line** at the beginning of *each* staff in the piece. This is called the **key signature**.

Key signature for G Major

These sharps mean to play all F's in the piece as **F-sharp**.

■ First, scan the music and circle all the *F-sharps*.

■ Practice the **R.H. alone** until you can play it easily. When you are ready, play hands together slowly.

Minuet in G

Christian Pezold
from the Notebook for
Anna Magdalena Bach
adapted

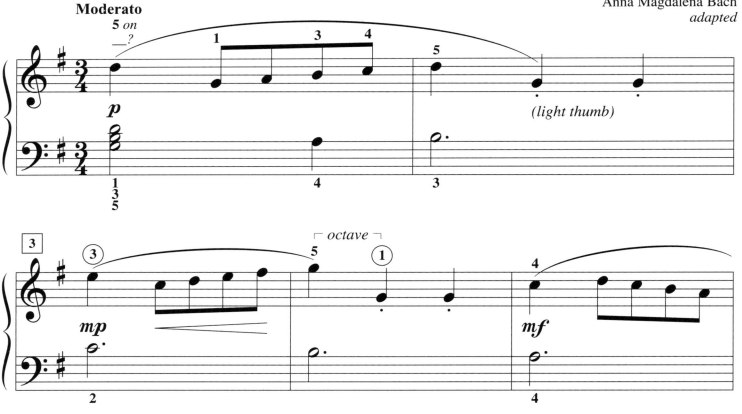

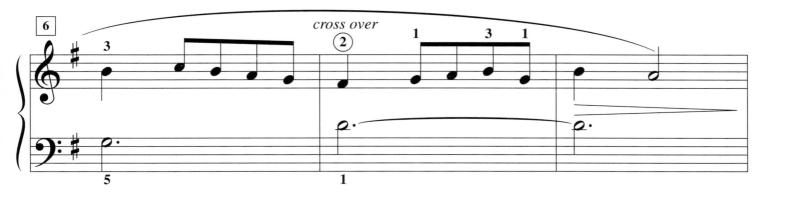

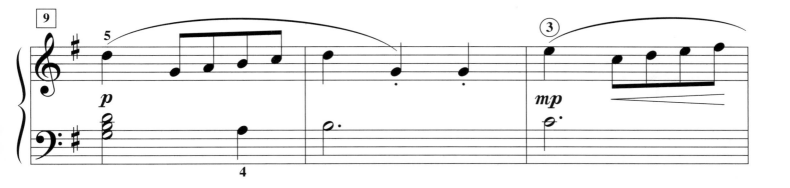

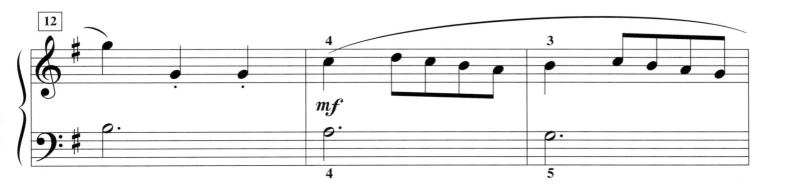

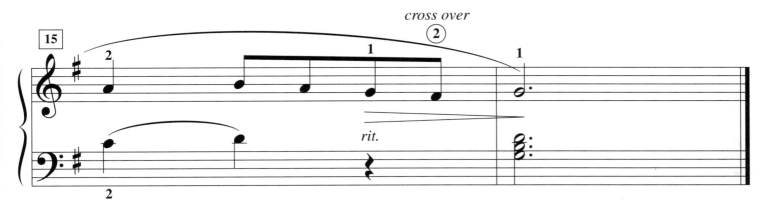

 DISCOVERY Point out at least two places where the *leading tone* moves up to the *tonic*.

PLAY VIDEO

- This piece opens with the G major scale divided between the left hand and right hand.

- The piece, almost entirely quarter notes, must be played with a steady, unwavering tempo.

Bells on a G Scale

Traditional

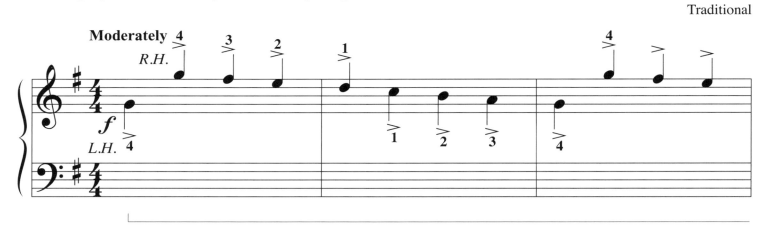

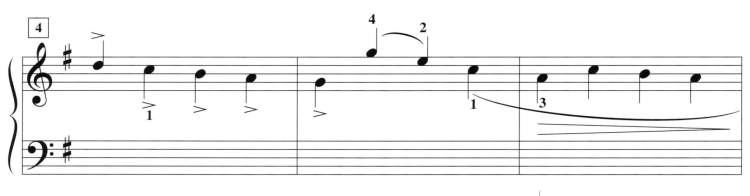

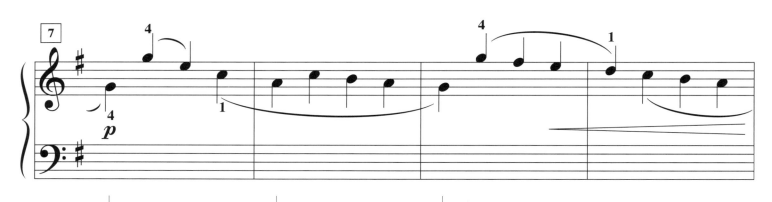

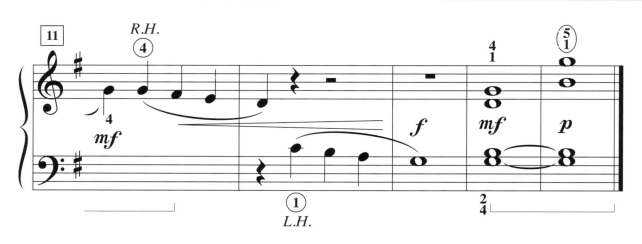

PLAY VIDEO

158

FF1302

1. Write the **R.H. fingering** for the G major scale below.
   Write **T** (tonic), **D** (dominant) or **LT** (leading tone) below the correct notes.
   Mark the *half steps* with a wedge (∨) below the notes.

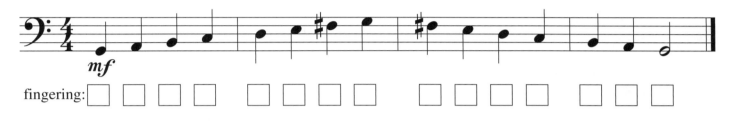

2. Now do the above three steps for the **L.H.** G major scale.

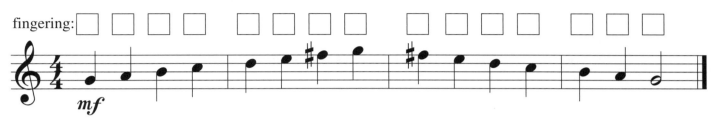

3. Circle each note that would be played as **F-sharp** in the music. Then *sightread* the music.
   Remember, this key signature means *all* F's **will be sharped.**

Close your eyes and listen. Your teacher (or a friend) will play a short example that will end on the *tonic, dominant,* or *leading tone*. Circle the correct answer. Note: Each example begins on the **tonic.**

a. tonic	**b.** tonic	**c.** tonic	**d.** tonic
dominant	dominant	dominant	dominant
leading tone	leading tone	leading tone	leading tone

For Teacher Use Only (The examples may be played in any order.)

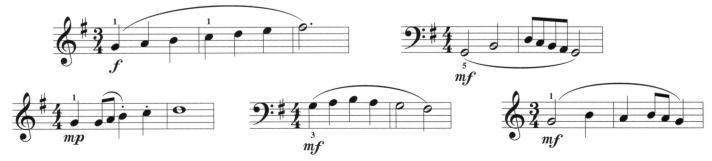

Primary Chords in G Major

D7 Chord in Root Position

The D7 chord is a four-note chord built up in **3rds** from **D**.
When D (the root) is the *lowest* note, the chord is in the ROOT POSITION.

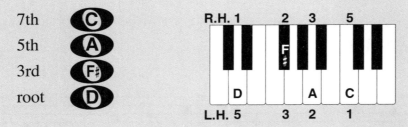

7th   C
5th   A
3rd   F♯
root   D

Inverted D7 Chord

The notes of the **D7** chord are often *inverted* (rearranged) to form a **3-note D7 chord**.

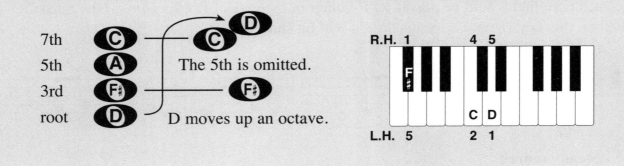

7th   C
5th   A   The 5th is omitted.
3rd   F♯
root   D   D moves up an octave.

D7 = V7 in the Key of G

Because D is *scale degree 5* (the dominant - V) in the Key of G, the **D7 chord** is called the
V7 ("five-seven") or **Dominant 7** chord in the Key of G.

Inverted D7 (V7) for L.H.

■ Play a 5th in the G major scale.

■ Move finger 5 a **half step lower** (F♯).
(This expands the interval to a 6th.)

■ Add **L.H. finger 2** (scale degree 4).

Inverted D7 (V7) for R.H.

■ Play a 5th in the G major scale.

■ Move finger 1 a **half step lower** (F♯).
(This expands the interval to a 6th.)

■ Add **R.H. finger 4** (scale degree 4).

Shift the R.H. "in" (toward the fallboard)
to easily play the black key (F♯).

PLAY VIDEO

Alexander March

Key of G Major

First play the R.H. alone rather slowly.

Observe the *staccatos* and *slurs*.

Ludwig van Beethoven
(1770-1827, Germany)
arranged

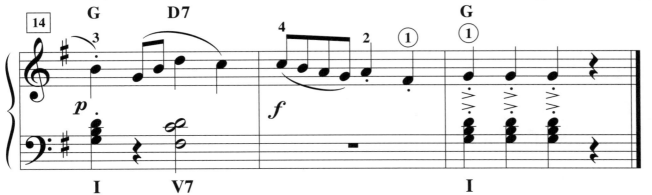

PLAY VIDEO

pianissimo (*pp*)

means very soft, softer than *piano*
(pronounced "pyah-NEES-see-moh")

Amazing Grace
Key of G Major

Words by John Newton
Early American melody
arranged

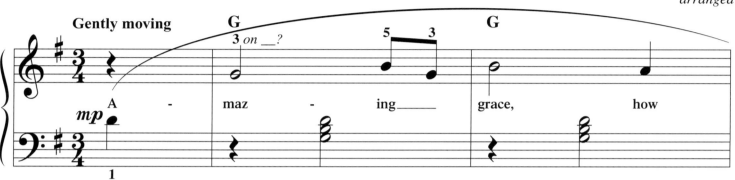

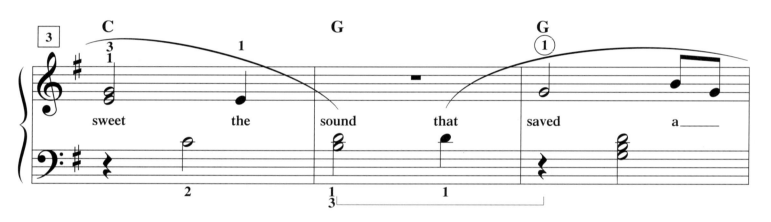

Teacher Duet: (Student plays *1 octave higher*, without pedal)

FF1302

 DISCOVERY Identify each chord as **I** or **V7** in *Amazing Grace*.

PLAY VIDEO

Inverting the IV Chord

Remember: The primary chords are built on steps 1, 4, and 5 of the major scale.

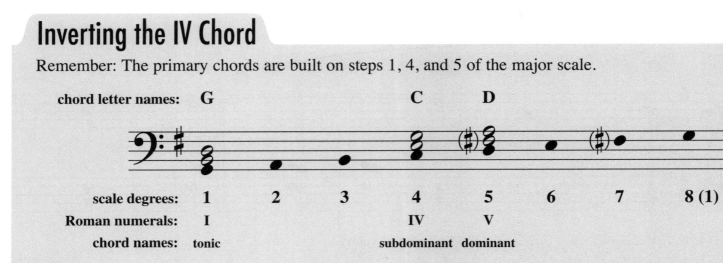

chord letter names:	G				C	D			

scale degrees:	1	2	3	4	5	6	7	8 (1)
Roman numerals:	I			IV	V			
chord names:	tonic			subdominant	dominant			

To eliminate the leap from the **I chord** to the **IV chord**, the notes of the IV chord can be rearranged, or inverted.

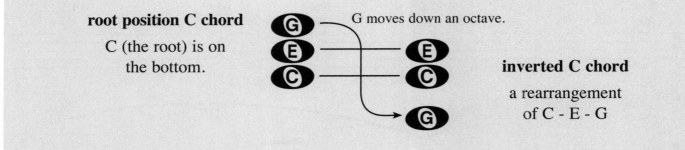

root position C chord

C (the root) is on the bottom.

G moves down an octave.

inverted C chord

a rearrangement of C - E - G

Inverted IV Chord for L.H.

- Finger 5 stays in the G major scale.

- The thumb moves UP a *whole step* (E).

- L.H. finger 2 plays C (scale degree 4).

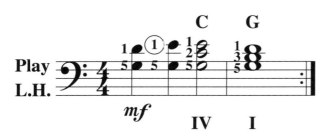

Inverted IV Chord for R.H.

- The thumb stays in the G major scale.

- Finger 5 moves UP a *whole step* (E).

- R.H. finger 3 moves up a *half step* to C (scale degree 4).

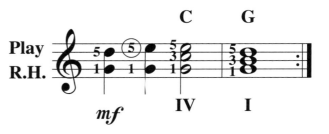

DISCOVERY Play a **G major pentascale** up and down s-l-o-w-l-y with your R.H.
Harmonize *each* note by playing a **G** (I), **C** (IV), or **D7** (V7) chord with your L.H.
Use *inversions* for the **C** and **D7** chords. Listen and let your ears guide you.

FF1302

IV Chord Warm-up in G

French Dance
Key of ____ Major

17th Century Melody
anonymous

1st and 2nd endings

| 1. | 2. |

Play the 1st ending and repeat from the beginning (or the facing repeat sign). Then play the 2nd ending, skipping the 1st ending.

descending G major scale

Write **I**, **IV**, or **V7** below each chord of *French Dance*.

PLAY VIDEO

Hint: Practice these two "tricky spots"
below playing hands together.

◼ 3rd finger cross-over at *measures 4–5*

◼ R.H. finger substitution at *measure 9*

Polovtsian Dance
(No. 17) (pronounced "pol-o-VETZ-ian")

Key of G Major

Alexander Borodin
(1833-1887, Russia)
arranged

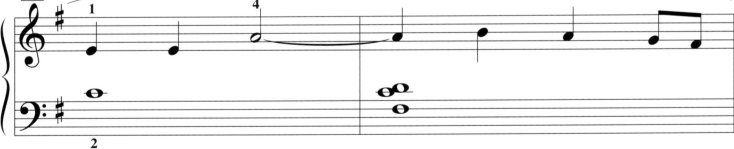

Teacher Duet: (Student plays *1 octave higher*, without pedal)

FF1302

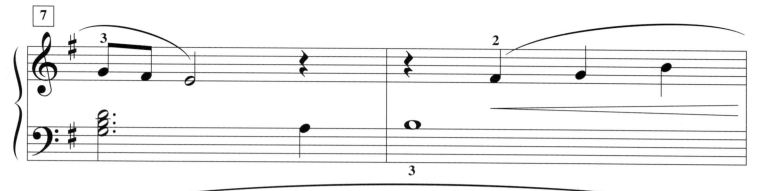

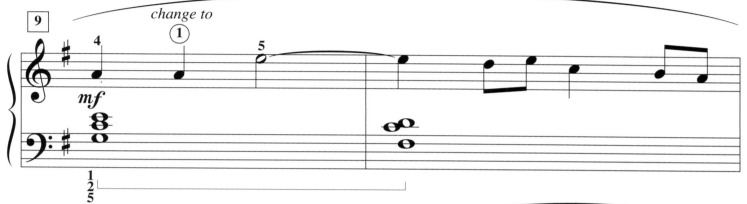

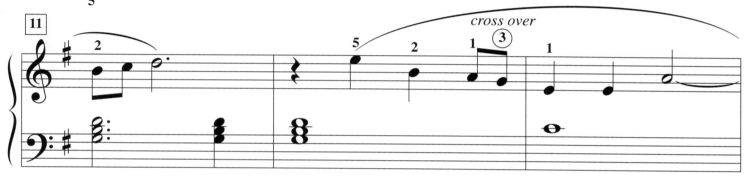

Point out the following in this piece:
phrase mark, tie, I chord, IV chord, V7 chord, *cresc.*, *dim.*, octave

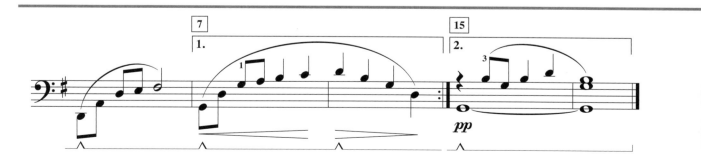

PLAY VIDEO

Lead Sheet in G Major

Now that you have learned the *primary chords* (I-IV-V7) in the Key of G major, explore playing the *melody* and *harmony* from a lead sheet in **G major**, following the directions below.

Chord References: Practice the chords used in *For He's a Jolly Good Fellow*.

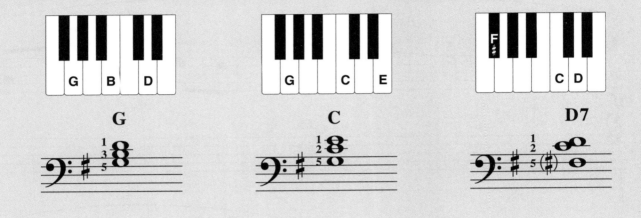

For He's a Jolly Good Fellow

■ First, play the melody only.

Traditional

■ Then add L.H. **blocked chords** on *beat 1 of each measure* as indicated by the chord symbols.

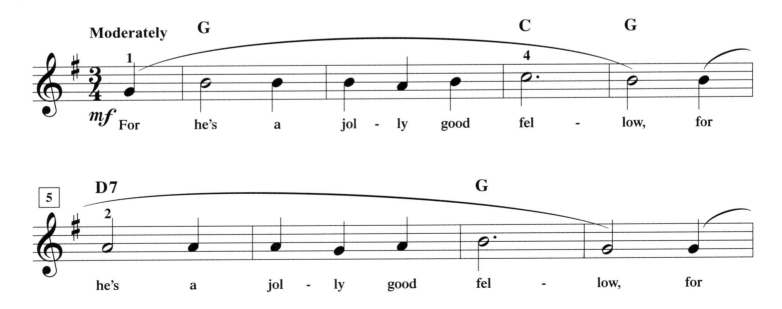

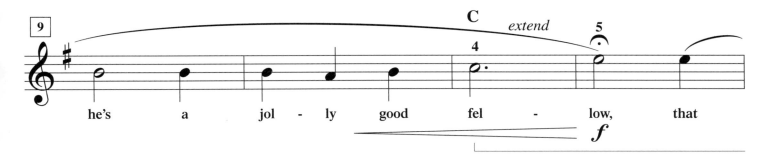

he's   a   jol - ly   good   fel - low,   that

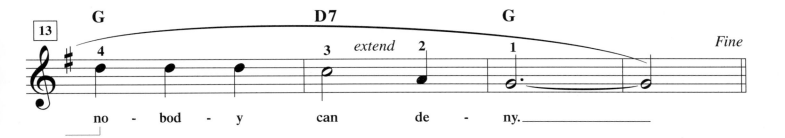

no - bod - y   can   de - ny._____

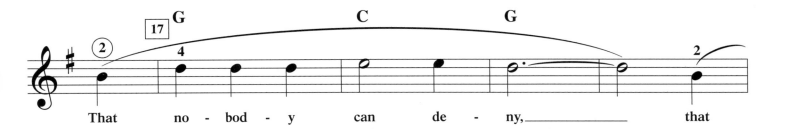

That   no - bod - y   can   de - ny,_____   that

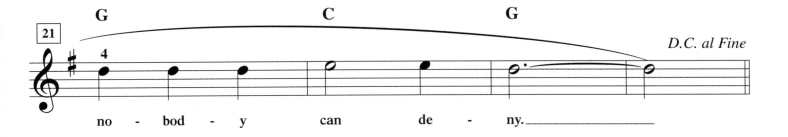

no - bod - y   can   de - ny._____

Banuwa (Village)

Folk Melody from Liberia

repeat!

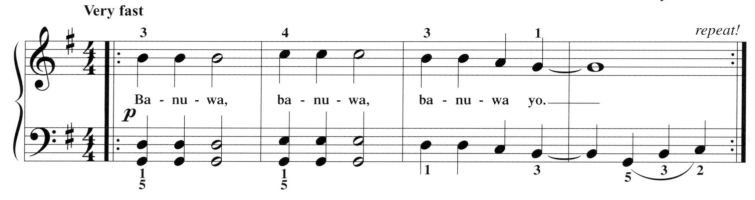

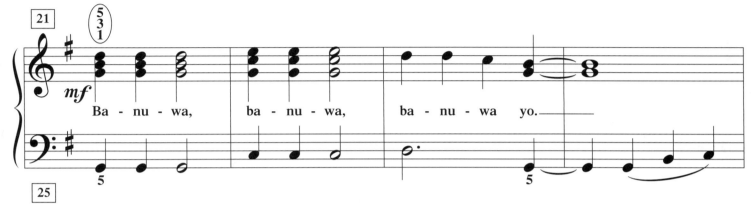

Ba - nu - wa, ba - nu - wa, ba - nu - wa yo.

Ba - nu - wa, ba - nu - wa, ba - nu - wa yo.

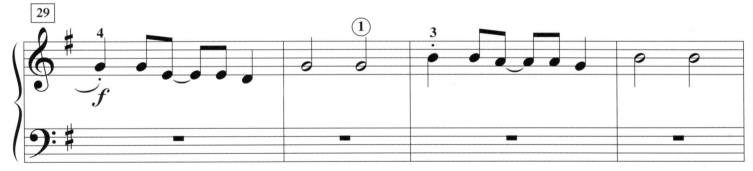

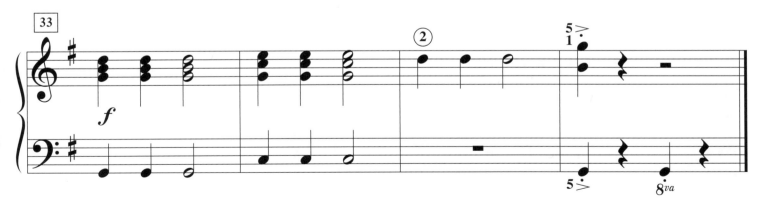

DISCOVERY Which two primary chords are used in this piece? **I**, **IV**, or **V7**

PLAY VIDEO

In this etude, each slur requires a gentle rolling gesture
from L.H. to R.H. for a smooth, connected sound.

Notice the R.H. always enters with the thumb.
Play it lightly for a flowing sound between the hands.

■ For a music box effect, play both hands 8va higher.

Music Box Etude
Key of ____ Major

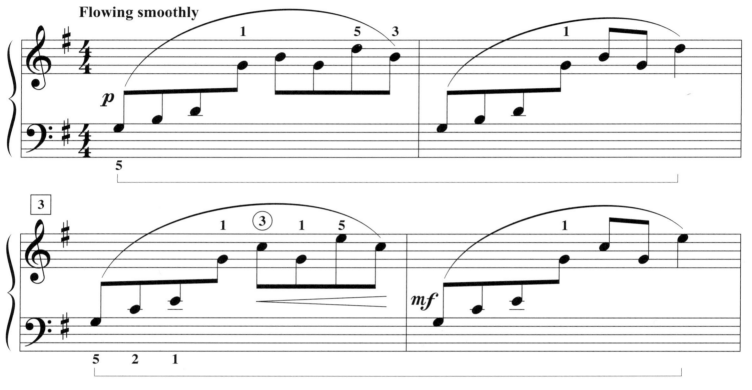

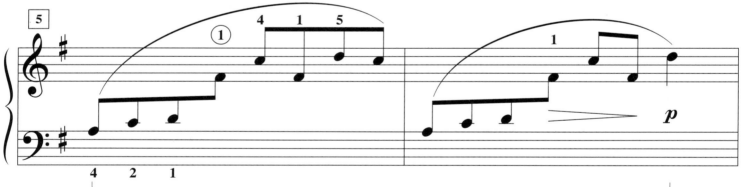

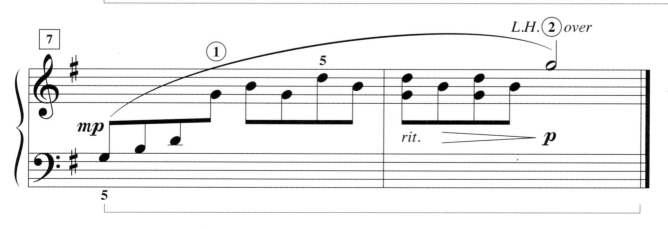

PLAY VIDEO

FF1302

Chord Progressions in C and G Major

1. Write the **chord letter names** and **Roman numerals** to complete the examples below.

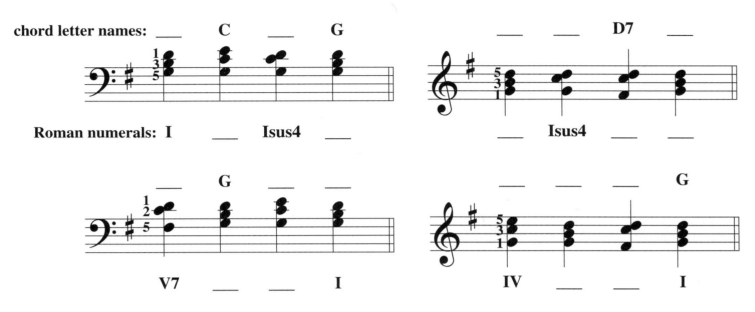

2. Now play all the chords written on the staves. Can you play hands together?

Your teacher (or a friend) will play one of the chord progressions above. Which chord progression did you hear?

Improvisation in G Major

- Your teacher (or a friend) will play the duet below. First, *listen* and feel the beat.

- When you are ready, improvise a melody using notes from the **G major scale** in any order, using *2nds* and *3rds*. Begin and end on **G** (the tonic).

Teacher Duet: (Student improvises *higher* on the keyboard)

The Carnival of Venice

(Carnivale di Venezia)

Key of _____ Major

Traditional Italian

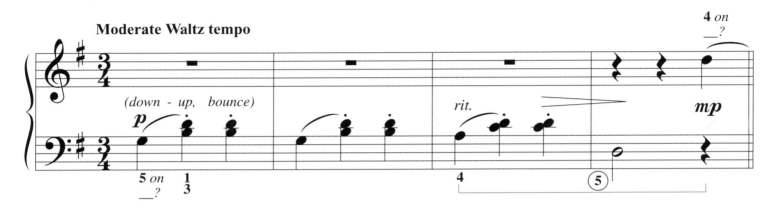

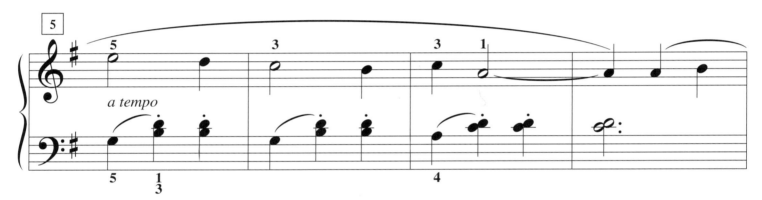

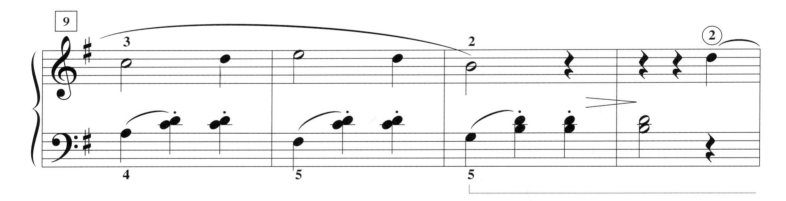

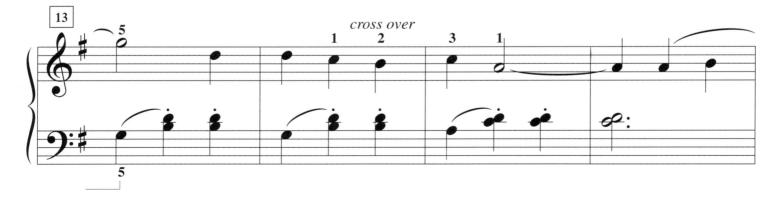

FF1302

The Carnival of Venice dates back to 1162 A.D.—over 800 years. St. Mark's Square was and still is the heart of the feast and celebration. The wearing of masks at the carnival has been hugely popular throughout the centuries. Apart from the style, fascination, and fun the masks offered, they also allowed people of different classes to mingle together. This traditional Italian melody has the carefree holiday spirit that surrounds the *Carnivale di Venezia*.

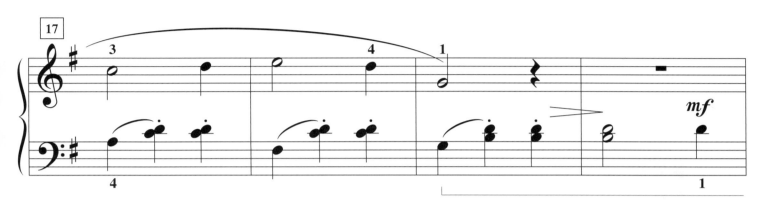

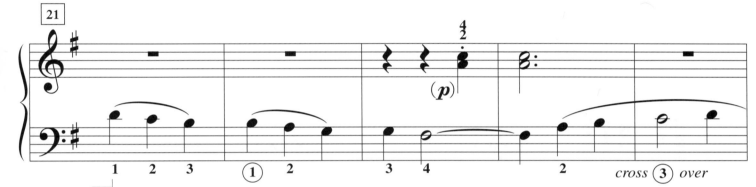

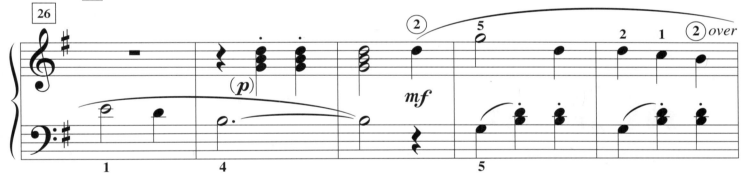

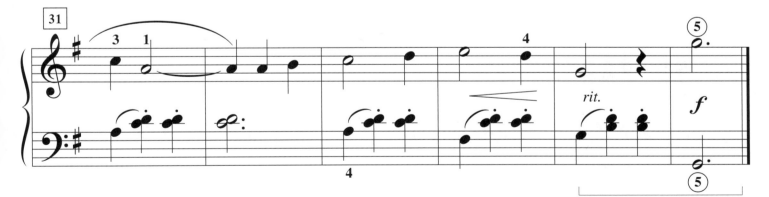

DISCOVERY Which two primary chords are used in this piece? **I**, **IV**, or **V7**

Congratulations! Your musical journey continues in **Adult Piano Adventures®** Course Book 2.

PLAY VIDEO

Major Pentascales

There are 12 major pentascales. You will benefit from learning and memorizing each.

H = Half Step   W = Whole Step

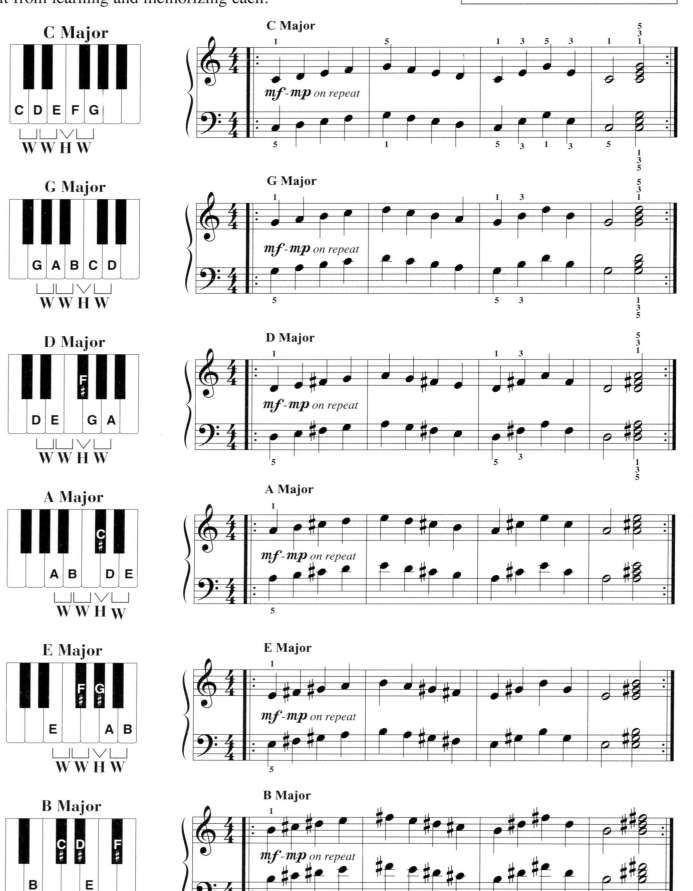

FF1302

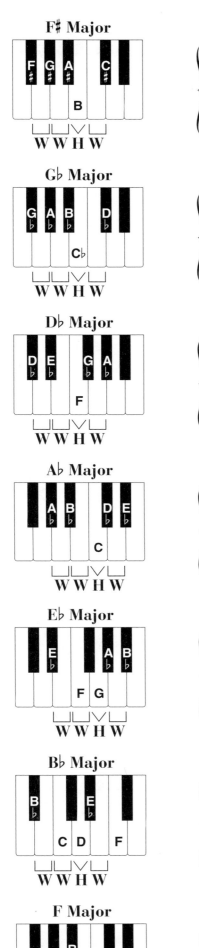

F♯ Major

W W H W

G♭ Major

W W H W

D♭ Major

W W H W

A♭ Major

W W H W

E♭ Major

W W H W

B♭ Major

W W H W

F Major

W W H W

F♯ Major

mf-mp on repeat

(also written as)

G♭ Major

mf-mp on repeat

D♭ Major

mf-mp on repeat

A♭ Major

mf-mp on repeat

E♭ Major

mf-mp on repeat

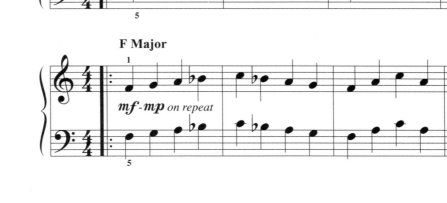

B♭ Major

mf-mp on repeat

F Major

mf-mp on repeat

Major Cross-Hand Arpeggios

There are 12 major cross-hand arpeggios. You will benefit from learning and memorizing each.

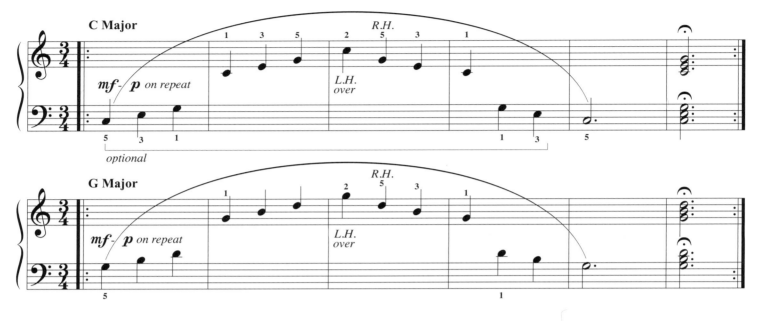

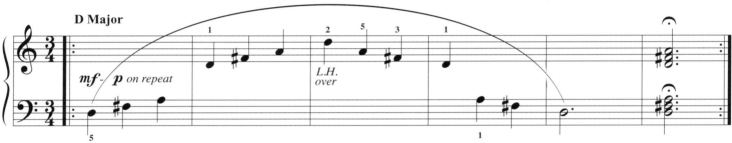

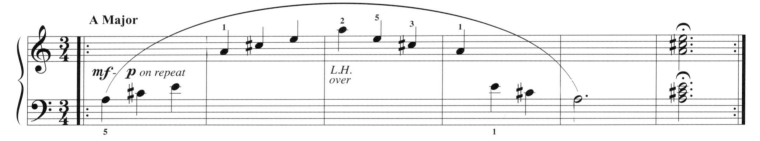

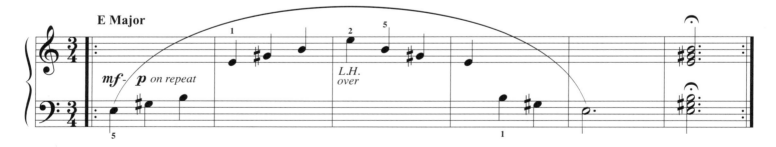

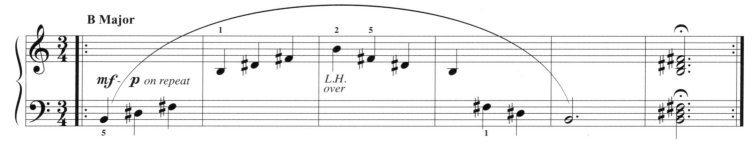

FF1302

G♭ Major

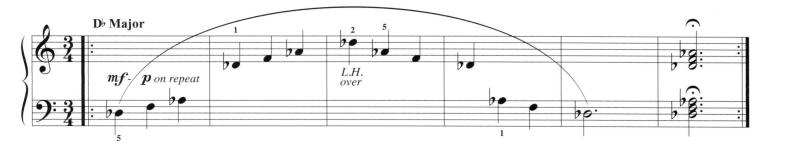

D♭ Major

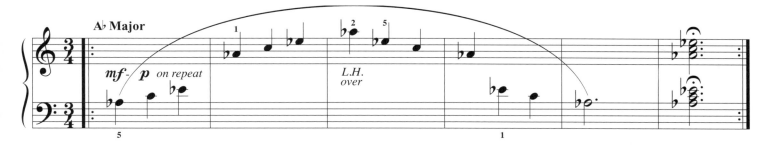

A♭ Major

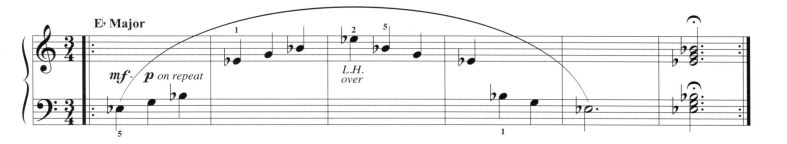

E♭ Major

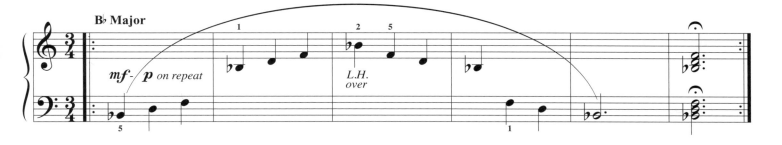

B♭ Major

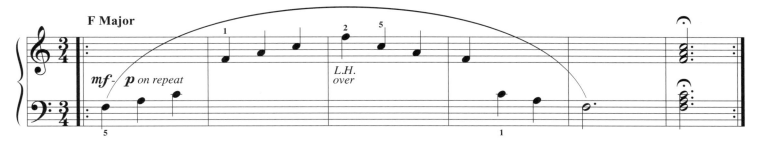

F Major

Dictionary

FF1302

DYNAMIC MARKS

pp	*p*	*mp*	*mf*	*f*
pianissimo	*piano*	*mezzo piano*	*mezzo forte*	*forte*
very soft	soft	moderately soft	moderately loud	loud

crescendo (cresc.)
Play gradually louder.

diminuendo (dim.) or decrescendo (decresc.)
Play gradually softer.

SIGN	TERM	DEFINITION
	accent mark	Play this note louder. (See p. 30)
	accidental	Sharps, flats, or naturals added to a piece and not in the key signature. (See p. 148)
	Allegro	Fast, lively tempo. (See p. 98)
	Andante	Walking tempo. (See p. 98)
	arpeggio	The notes of a chord played one after another, going up or down. (See pp. 88, 178)
	bar line	A line which divides the music into measures. (See p. 21)
	bass clef	The bass clef is used to show lower notes and is usually on the bottom staff. It is also called the F clef because the two dots point out the F line. (See pp. 29, 46)
	blocked	The tones of a chord or interval played together. (See pp. 18, 142)
	broken	The tones of a chord or interval played separately. (See pp. 18, 23, 116, 142)
	C major chord	A three-note chord built in 3rds above C: C-E-G. (See pp. 56, 76, 142, 164)
	C major scale	An eight-note scale (C-D-E-F-G-A-B-C) with half steps between scale steps 3-4 and 7-8. (See pp. 128–129)
	C pentascale	Five notes stepping up from C: C-D-E-F-G. (See pp. 22, 42, 62, 90)
	can-can	A lively 19th-century French dance that features high kicks performed by women in a chorus line. (See p. 136)
	chord	Three or more tones sounding together. (See p. 56)
	I ("one") chord	Three notes built up in 3rds from the tonic note. (See pp. 142, 144, 160)
	IV ("four")	Three notes built up in 3rds from the fourth note of the scale. (See pp. 142, 144, 164)
	V7 ("five-seven")	A four-note chord built up in 3rds from the dominant note (scale degree 5), often played with only three notes. (See pp. 134, 160)
	chord symbol	The letter name of a chord, written above the treble staff, which indicates the harmony. (See p. 77)
	coda	Ending section. (See p. 45)
	contrary motion	Two musical lines moving in opposite directions at the same time. (See pp. 68, 129, 155)

	crescendo	Play gradually louder. (See p. 72)
	Csus4 chord	The 3 tones of the Csus4 chord are C-F-G. The Csus4 chord uses the 4th note (F) in place of the 3rd note (E) to give a suspended feeling to this chord. (See p. 77)
	D7 chord	A four-note chord built up in 3rds from D (D-F♯-A-C). The notes of the D7 chord are often inverted to form a 3-note D7 chord. (See p. 160)
D.C. al Fine	**Da Capo al Fine**	Return to the beginning and play until Fine (end). (See p. 55)
	damper pedal	The right pedal, which sustains the sound, played with the right foot. (See pp. 6, 11)
	decrescendo	Play gradually softer. (See p. 72)
	diminuendo	Play gradually softer. (See p. 72)
	dominant	Scale degree 5 of a scale. (See pp. 128, 134, 142, 160)
	dotted half note	Three counts or beats. (See p. 14)
	double bar line	A thin, then thick bar line indicating the end of a piece. (See p. 15)
	dynamics	The "louds and softs" of music. See dynamic markings at the top of page 180. (See pp. 10, 26, 71)
	eighth notes	Two eighth notes equal one quarter note. (See p. 70)
	etude	A piece of music for the development of a certain technical skill. (See pp. 152, 172)
	F major chord	A three-note chord built in 3rds above F: F A C. F is the root. A is the 3rd. C is the 5th. (See p. 86)
	fermata	Hold this note longer than its normal value. (See p. 75)
	fifth (5th)	The interval of a 5th spans five letter names. (Ex. C up to G, or A down to D) Line-(skip-a-line)-line, or space-(skip-a-space)-space. (See pp. 116, 120)
	finger substitution	Changing to a new finger on a repeated note. (See p. 136)
	1st and 2nd endings	Play the 1st ending and repeat from the beginning (or the facing repeat sign). Then play the 2nd ending, skipping over the 1st ending. (See p. 165)
♭	**flat**	A flat lowers a note one half step. (See p. 108)
f	*forte*	Loud (See p. 10)
ff	*fortissimo*	Very loud.
	fourth (4th)	The interval of a 4th spans four letter names. (Ex. C up to F, or A down to E) Line-(skip-a-line)-space, or space-(skip-a-space)-line. (See pp. 116–117)
	G major chord	A three-note chord built in 3rds above G: G B D. G is the root. B is the 3rd. D is the 5th. (See pp. 100, 168)
	G major scale	An eight-note scale (G-A-B-C-D-E-F♯-G) with half steps between scale degrees 3-4 and 7-8. (See pp. 154–155)
	G pentascale	Five notes stepping up from G: G-A-B-C-D. (See pp. 25, 96–97)
	G7 chord	A four-note chord built up in 3rds from G (G-B-D-F). The notes of the G7 chord are often inverted to form a 3-note G7 chord. (See p. 134)

SIGN	TERM	DEFINITION
	gavotte	A lively French dance in $\frac{4}{4}$ time. It usually begins with two upbeats. (See p. 77)
	grand staff	Two staves connected by a bar and brace, used for keyboard music. (See p. 28)
	Gsus4 chord	The 3 tones of the Gsus4 chord are G-C-D. (See p. 100)
	half note	Two counts or beats (one-half the value of a whole note). (See p. 14)
	half rest	Two counts of silence. (Sits on line 3 of the staff) (See p. 58)
	half step	The distance from one key to the very closest key on the keyboard. (Ex. D-E♭, or E-F) (See pp. 104, 114)
	harmony	Notes or chords played along with the melody. (See p. 54)
	imitation	The immediate repetition of a musical idea played by the other hand. (See pp. 91, 94)
	improvisation	To make up or compose music "on the spot," without preparation. (See pp. 27, 49, 69, 89, 133, 173)
	interval	The distance between two musical tones, keys on the keyboard, or notes on the staff. (Ex. 2nd, 3rd, 4th, 5th) (See pp. 18, 22, 23, 34, 50, 57, 61, 116–117, 120, 122)
	inversion	Rearranging the notes of a chord. Ex. C-E-G may invert to E-G-C or G-C-E. (See pp. 134, 144, 160, 164)
	key signature	The key signature appears at the beginning of each line of music. It indicates sharps or flats to be used throughout the piece. (See p. 156)
	lead sheet	The melody only with chord symbols written above the staff. (See pp. 150, 168)
	**leading tone**	Scale degree 7 of a scale. (See pp. 128, 154)
	ledger line	A short line used to extend the staff. (See pp. 29, 78, 112)
	legato	Smooth, connected. (See p. 38)
	**major pentascale**	A five-note scale formed by this pattern of whole steps (W) and half-steps (H): W W H W (See pp. 114, 115, 176, 177)
	**major scale**	An eight-note scale with half steps between scale degrees 3-4 and 7-8. (See pp. 128, 154)
	march	A piece in $\frac{2}{4}$ or $\frac{4}{4}$ time, characterized by a strong rhythmic beat. (See p. 161)
	measure	Music is divided into groups of beats called measures. Each measure has an equal number of beats. (See p. 21)
	melody	The tune. (See pp. 32, 54)
	metronome	A rhythm device that ticks a steady beat. Adjustable settings allow a faster or slower beat. (See pp. 14, 129, 155)
mf	*mezzo forte*	Moderately loud (See p. 26)
mp	*mezzo piano*	Moderately soft (See p. 71)
	minuet (menuet)	A stately dance in $\frac{3}{4}$ time. (See pp. 71, 156)
	Moderato	Moderate tempo (See p. 98)

	musette	A lively piece imitating the sound of a bagpipe. (See p. 98)
	music alphabet	A-B-C-D-E-F-G. These letters repeated over and over, name the keys on the piano and notes on the grand staff. (See p. 16)
	musical form	The overall structure or plan of a piece. (See pp. 24, 36, 44, 46, 59)
	musical pattern	A short rhythmic and melodic set of notes. (See p. 26)
♮	**natural**	A natural (always a white key) cancels a sharp or a flat. (See p. 110)
	octave	The interval which spans 8 letter names. (Ex. C to C) (See pp. 40, 64, 96)
8va – ⌐	*ottava*	Play one octave higher (or lower) than written. (See p. 40)
	parallel motion	Two musical lines moving in the same direction at the same time. (See pp. 68, 129)
	pedal mark	Shows the down-up motion of the damper pedal. (See p. 33)
	pentascale	See major pentascale.
	phrase	A musical sentence. A phrase is often shown by a slur, also called a phrase mark. (See p. 72)
pp	*pianissimo*	Very soft. (See p. 162)
p	*piano*	Soft, quiet. (See p. 10)
	pick-up note, upbeat	The note(s) of an incomplete opening measure. (See p. 74)
	pitch	The highness or lowness of a tone (sound). (See p. 10)
	primary chords	The I, IV, and V chords are the primary chords in any major key. (See pp. 142, 164)
	promenade	A slow, dignified march of the guests at the opening of an important event. (See p. 117)
♩	**quarter note**	One count or beat. (One-quarter the value of a whole note.) (See p. 14)
𝄽	**quarter rest**	One beat of silence. (See p. 52)
15ma – ⌐	**quindicessima**	Play two octaves higher (or lower) than written. (See p. 40)
𝄆 𝄇	**repeat sign**	Play the music within the repeat signs again. (See pp. 16, 65)
	repeated note	A note on the same line or space as the preceding note. (See p. 19)
	rhythm	Music has short, medium, and long notes. Counting the duration of each note using a steady beat (or pulse) creates rhythm. (See p. 14)
rit.	*ritardando*	Gradually slowing down. (See pp. 66, 92)
	root position	The letter name of the chord is the lowest note. (See pp. 134, 142, 160, 164)
	scale	From the Latin word scala, meaning "ladder." The notes of a scale move up or down by 2nds (steps). (See pp. 22, 128, 154)
	second (2nd) (step)	The interval that spans two letter names. (Ex. C up to D, or F down to E) On the staff: line-to-the-next-space or space-to-the-next-line. (See pp. 22, 34)
	sequence	A musical pattern repeated at a higher or lower pitch. (See pp. 26, 60)

SIGN	TERM	DEFINITION
♯	**sharp**	A sharp raises the note one half step. (See p. 104)
	sightread	Playing through a piece for the very first time (at sight). (See p. 41)
	sixth (6th)	The interval that spans six letter names. (Ex. E up to C, or A down to C) On the staff a 6th is written line-(skip 2 lines)-space or space-(skip 2 spaces)-line. (See p. 122)
	slur	A curved line that indicates legato playing. (See p. 38)
	staccato	Detached, disconnected. (See p. 64)
	staff	The five lines and four spaces on which notes are written. (See p. 28)
sus4	**suspended-4 chord**	A three-note chord that uses the 4th instead of the 3rd. (See pp. 77, 100)
	symphony	A long composition for orchestra usually consisting of three or four related movements. (See pp. 24, 54, 64)
	tempo	The speed of the music. (See pp. 48, 100)
	theme	A principal melody, often made of several phrases. (See pp. 24, 54, 64, 84, 100)
	third (3rd) (skip)	The interval that spans three letter names. (Ex. C up to E, or F down to D) On the staff: line-to-the-next-line or space-to-the-next-space. (See pp. 19, 23, 50)
	tie	A curved line that connects two notes on the same line or space. Hold for the total counts of both notes. (See p. 35)
2/4 3/4 4/4	**time signature**	Two numbers at the beginning of a piece (one above the other). The top number indicates the number of beats per measure; the bottom number represents the note receiving the beat. (See pp. 30–31)
	tonic	Scale degree 1 of a scale. The tone on which a scale is built. (See pp. 128, 154)
	transpose	To play music in a different key. (See p. 20)
	treble clef	The treble clef is used to show higher notes and is usually on the top staff. It is also called the G clef because it circles around the G line. (See pp. 29, 42)
	triad	A 3-note chord built in 3rds. (See pp. 56, 76)
	upbeat (pick-up note)	The note(s) of an incomplete opening measure. (See p. 74)
	waltz	A dance piece in 3/4 time. (See pp. 110, 132, 138)
o	**whole note**	Four counts or beats. (See p. 14)
	whole rest	Silence for any whole measure. (Hangs below line 4) (See p. 58)
	whole step	The distance of two half steps. (See p. 112)